THE MOVIE BUSINESS

THE MOVIE BUSINESS

DAVID LEES AND

STAN BERKOWITZ

VINTAGE BOOKS · A DIVISION OF RANDOM HOUSE · NEW YORK

A Vintage Books Original, April 1981
First Edition
Copyright © 1978, 1979, 1980, 1981 by David Lees
& Stan Berkowitz
All rights reserved under International
and Pan-American Copyright Conventions. Published
in the United States by Random House, Inc., New
York, and simultaneously in Canada by Random
House of Canada Limited, Toronto.

Portions of this work have originally appeared in
Los Angeles magazine and the Los Angeles *Times*.

Library of Congress Cataloging in Publication Data
Lees, David, 1950–
The movie business.
1. Moving–picture industry—United States.
I. Berkowitz, Stan, 1949–   II. Title.
PN1993.5.U6L42   384'.8'0973   80–6141
ISBN 0–394–74666–x   AACR2

Manufactured in the United States of America

"Critics have lots of ways of telling us what is a good movie. They have stars or cherries, or other ways to tell us. But, as businessmen, we have only one gauge for a good movie. How much money did it make?"

—*Andy Albeck*
President, United Artists

There was much concern among committee members, who cited their purpose as being a business and economic one, with no cultural significance attached.

—*A report on the Los Angeles Film Development Council*, Hollywood Reporter

ACKNOWLEDGMENTS

MANY PEOPLE THROUGHOUT THE FILM INDUSTRY GAVE GENEROUSLY OF their time in the preparation of this book. Although we regret that we cannot acknowledge all of them, thanks are especially due Merv Adelson, Lorimar; Jane Alsobrook; Robert Altman; Alex Auerbach; Les Barnum; John Baron; Craig Baumgartner, Paramount; Jay Bernstein; Marcie Bollatin, Paramount; Stan Breitbard; Clayton Brown; Mitchell Cannold, Noah's Ark; Alan Carr; Kathy Clark, Disney; Chuck Codol, Paramount; Sheldon Cohen, IRS; Patrick Curtis; Robert Eisenbach, Eisenbach and Greene; Ed Elbert; Don Enright; J. Fleming, Disney; Hy Foreman, Paramount; Burt Forester; Kathy Foster; Menahem Golan, Canon Films; Hilton Green, Universal; Helene Hahn, Paramount; Bill Harvey; Bob Holmes, 20th Century-Fox; Bill Howard; Joe Hyams, Warners; Irv Ivers, 20th Century-Fox; John Jurgens; Douglas Kramer; John Landis; Jennings Lang, Universal; Charles Lippincott; Bob Levinson, Levinson and Associates; Barry Lorie, Associated Film Distributors; Seb Manno; Mike Maslansky, Maslansky Konisberg; Russ Meyer; Meyer Mishkin; Edward Montoro, Film Ventures International; John Morrissey; Booker McClay, Universal; Chuck Napier;

Michael O'Connor; Tim Penland; David Picker, Lorimar; Charles Powell; Bob Proctor, Paramount; Barry Reardon, Warners; Lee Rich, Lorimar; Ed Roginski, Universal; Jeff Schultz; Jack Schwartzman, Lorimar; Walter Senior; Stuart Shapiro; Norbert Simmons, MCA-New Ventures; Fred Skidmore, Warners; Richard St. Johns, Guinness Film Group Ltd.; Tommy Thompson; Stephen Traxler; Elsie Wallace; Lynn Weissman, 20th Century-Fox; Stan White, 20th Century-Fox; Robert Wilkinson, Universal; James Woods.

Additionally, we wish to thank Irv Letofsky and Wayne Warga of the Los Angeles *Times* for their occasional advice. Brian Weiss, Gail Winston, and Glenn Cowley each in his or her own way made this book possible. A special debt of gratitude is also due Stephen Randall, Sid Kahn, Irene Bagge, Toni Jackson, and Brenda Austin for their continuing help or suggestions. Finally, to our parents, for their support, we are also thankful.

PREFACE

THIS BOOK WILL PROVIDE YOU WITH A CLEAR PICTURE OF THE WAY Hollywood works. Not only will we look at how movie deals are initiated and how movies are distributed and exhibited, but we'll see what part personalities play in this highly idiosyncratic business.

We have chosen to view movies mainly from the economic perspective. Our questions seemed obvious at times: Where does the money come from, what channels does it go through, and what sort of money do film people make? But we quickly learned that these were questions that had never really been explored. The film business, in which illusion is so important, likes to conceal its day-to-day realities.

It is, however, with some trepidation that we discuss movies and money, especially in a book geared to the general reader. Money usually acts as a magnet; stories of quick fortunes have drawn thousands of hopefuls to Hollywood, all in search of a big screenplay sale or an even bigger production deal. By publicizing the relatively few instances of spectacular overnight success, the show business press, knowingly or unwittingly, inspires thousands of individuals who otherwise aren't interested in movies. And despite glib assertions from a number of moviemakers that they're only in it for the money, that motivation is not enough and never has been.

Creativity—something new, something different—or perhaps a writer or director's sincere commitment to his material—these are things that cannot be faked, no matter how much money is spent to make a film. Without at least a glimmer of those two elements, a film will almost certainly be rejected by the public. Someone with nothing but money on his mind may very well become an instant success, but for most there will be years of waiting, a time when some sort of artistic vision is needed to sustain hope.

That hope—for a creative and financial jackpot—is something that looms larger in the eyes of outsiders than it does within the industry. The movie industry offers about as much certainty to its participants as the racetrack, but like the track's professional gamblers, people in the film business manage to survive. Everything they do can ultimately be seen in terms of risk management, from spreading their bets among several different projects to making sequels of films that have already proven themselves in the marketplace. And it should be pointed out that survival doesn't always mean homes in Beverly Hills and a Mercedes Benz. Although there's a tight bond between a successful career and the appearance of status in Hollywood, only a small (but highly visible) percentage of the film community wallows in excess. The rest —moderately successful writers, actors with familiar faces, directors of photography, lab employees—live on middle-class incomes, and some subsist on less.

This book began in articles we wrote for *Los Angeles* magazine, *Box Office,* and the Los Angeles *Times.* From that beginning we have added considerable new material and updated the originals. Our sources are numerous and quite varied. Only a few asked that their names not be mentioned or that things they told us not be printed. When we did run into off-the-record information, we tried to use it anyway but in such a way as to keep the source unidentified. In most cases our sources' names are not household words outside the film community, so we often refer to them by just their titles.

We found a high degree of cooperation among our interview subjects—surprising in that none of them had a thing to gain by answering our questions. Only four prospective interviewees among hundreds declined to talk, citing time pressures as their reason. Those who did take time out for us have our gratitude.

CONTENTS

INTRODUCTION

WHEN WE BEGAN WRITING ABOUT MOVIES, WE BUMPED INTO A FUNDA-
mental fact about the way things work in Hollywood.

We found out that movies are primarily a business deal. Movies can
be a lot of other things at the same time: cultural artifact, personal
statement, or an experience that entertains and enlightens in a way
unavailable in any other medium.

But movies are all or any of these things only because somebody
somewhere provided the money to get them made, in exchange for a
potential economic benefit of some sort.

Like many other people who make a discovery that seems both novel
and obvious at the same time, we were pretty pleased with ourselves.
All we had to do, we figured, was to go down to the local bookstore,
check out the shelves labeled "film" or "cinema," and read up on how
the business works. After that the riddles, contradictions, and all the
things that seem so natural to those in the business and so strange to
the rest of us would all be resolved. We decided, too, that we were
more interested in learning a little more about the people who make
the decisions affecting the fate of the celebrities than we were in

merely finding out about the hobbies, zodiac sign, or favorite restaurant of the celebrities themselves.

We live in Los Angeles, and—say what you like about the place—there are plenty of good bookstores around. Many of them specialize in lore about Hollywood. We were on our way to solving the puzzle of how things work in what people alternately call "the Industry" or "this crazy business."

We found film histories. We thumbed through lavish memoirs of the famous and their friends, along with biographies both authorized and scandalous. There were tomes about film theory and film scripts of the masters impressively annotated, illustrated, and anthologized. "Novelizations" of hit films and even cutout books devoted to the young and usually uninteresting life of the current teen audience idol were lumped together on the movie shelf.

We began to feel a little uneasy. Our obvious discovery didn't seem so obvious. There just weren't any books around on the workings of the movie business. There were a lot of how-to books, each promising that the investment of a few dollars in cold cash and a few hours of reading time would show the buyer how to write a screenplay or how to make a movie. That wasn't what we were after. We had already learned that the business wouldn't be half so bizarre—or half so interesting—if there were a set of steps for success anybody could follow as if it were a diet. Besides, most of the people we met who were qualified to write a book spelling out the ingredients of success were too busy making movies to write books.

There was nothing to do except to start poking around the business for ourselves, asking the kind of questions anybody would who is interested in how things work.

About two years ago we noticed that other people were starting to talk about the business side of things in Hollywood. It began slowly enough, but it has snowballed to the point that today, as we write, talking about the inside story of specific film deals has become a kind of new gossip, threatening to replace the more traditional concern with the lives of the people who grace magazine covers and take up time on the talk shows.

As gossip, talk about the business side of films has three things going for it right away. Like any sort of hot chat, it singles out the people who are doing the talking as privy to inside information denied to others. And gossip about business in Hollywood is still gossip about Hollywood. The money, the power, the personalities all share an exaggerated scale of dimensions that tends to make tales about them naturally tall.

Finally, talking about the business of movies entails the ability to throw around a lot of seemingly technical words, an arcane language that only confirms the insider status of those doing the talking.

The trouble is, none of this talk about the economic arrangements of the movie business makes any sense unless it's anchored to some understanding of the mechanisms those buzzwords are supposed to describe.

Movie critics and professors of film theory aren't much help in getting a handle on the new interest in the business of movies. Perhaps fearing that their lock on the last word about films will be loosened— reviews are part of the old gossip about film, grosses at the box office belong squarely to the new—critics and theorists have lately published long essays and ponderous volumes that center around the idea that movies are worse than ever because of the way the business is set up. Change the format of the business and the kind of movies these critics are wont to go ape for will magically emerge, they say.

But movies are probably no better or no worse than they have ever been. Any art, from painting to publishing, has produced in any given year a pile of mediocre work. Interest in a particular artistic enterprise is leavened by the works that stand out, not by the commonplace. And that's why the standouts stand out.

There is another problem, too, in mixing art and commerce when talking about films. Movies, it is worthwhile to say again, are a business deal, a collection of economic decisions. The production of a movie is a collection of artistic and logistical judgments, exercised in collaboration by the director or producer with the cast and crew. The goal of the deal and the goal of the production overlap only accidentally. The studio executive may be concerned with how good a movie might be, but his primary task and responsibility is to maximize profits. A director can reasonably be expected to hope that the movie under his supervision will make money, but his job is to do the best job with what he has. Sometimes, the goals of commerce intersect with the goals of art, sometimes not. It all depends upon the film in question.

Less conglomeration or more, smaller budgets or larger, will only result in an increase or decrease—perhaps—in the number of films produced. There is no guarantee that they will be any better. Any year in anyone's appointed Golden Age of Movies had film cans full of junk delivered to the movie houses along with the classics.

So, we decided that *The Movie Business* ought to concentrate on an explanation of how the economics of moviemaking operates, looked at more or less apart from the aesthetic effects of those operations.

In *The Movie Business* there are two ways we try to arrive at that explanation. The primary goal of each of the chapters is to outline the more important chores usually involved in deciding how films are made and marketed. Beyond that we also explore the central role played by uncertainty in determining the character of most of the decision making that goes on before and after the cameras have rolled.

The plain fact is that just as movies are fundamentally the result of an interlocking set of economic decisions, so, too, are those decisions carried out against a backdrop of chance. To our way of thinking, the position of chance as a motivating factor sets the business of movies apart from almost any other economic enterprise. There are no statistical norms to measure performance, no way to be assured that forward fiscal planning will ever pan out, and no way to draw up a set of specifications for a hit movie. Everybody has heard stories of the sure smash that bombed or the sleeper that broke all attendance records at the box office.

"Nobody knows what makes a hit" is the official mantra of the movie business; the uncertainty engendered by this shaky state of affairs causes, quite naturally, a parallel sense of anxiety about decision making. There are no guidelines to consult that will indicate anything other than approximate probability. Research and development is nonexistent. Product testing takes place only after the film has hit the streets. By then it is too late.

The mechanisms we describe in *The Movie Business* can be seen not only as techniques for manufacturing and distributing films as a product but, more usefully, as ways to manage uncertainty.

After the initial chapters, which describe some of the duties of the people who work behind the scenes, we move into a discussion of budgeting production costs, an arithmetical activity that nevertheless entails a degree of chance. Next, we examine the three major arenas of the business—studios, "mini-majors," and independents. We explain how they are set up and how they work, as well as the evolution of their different strategies for coping with uncertainty.

The following set of chapters deals with the complex ins and outs developed to market and finance films. Our concluding chapter discusses the advent of new technologies and deals with a new era of filmmaking in which it appears that for the first time capital may exceed the needs of production, making the movies into a surefire profit machine matched only by the telephone company or OPEC.

We rely on interview throughout *The Movie Business*. While we have never intended the book to be in any major sense a how-to book, we are concerned with the way things work on a practical level rather than on a theoretical plane. It seemed to us that if we wanted to know how things are done, we ought to make sure to ask people who do them every day. We offer these opinions from people who have widely divergent perspectives. We leave it to the reader to triangulate a version of what may be the truth from the connection of the differing viewpoints presented here.

Finally, we think we owe the reader a brief discussion of our perspective and prejudices in putting together this book. Our basic stance during the years we have been covering the business of movies for publications in this country and abroad has been to consider ourselves outsiders. At first we had little choice in the matter. Later we decided to stick with it. We take very little for granted, even less on faith. Like anyone who has studied Hollywood, we are ambivalent toward what goes on there. There are many courageous production executives working at studios, mini-majors, or independently who have the refreshing audacity to commit millions of others people's money to a new idea. Just the same, there has never been a case where anyone in the business came to any harm by saying no to an idea. A continuing climate of uncertainty tends to breed conservatism on the part of those who have to watch the weather.

The idea that the movies are a tough business is no cliché. There is a lot of stress, and a lot of institutionalized cruelty, in a business where the privotal place of chance carries with it a chilling consequence. In the movie business it isn't a question of whether or not people know what they're doing but whether or not they *can* know.

This book is dedicated to those people who do the best they can anyway.

THE MOVIE BUSINESS

CREDITS:
THE NAME GAME

ONE OF THE MORE VOLATILE MIXES IN THE FILM BUSINESS COMBINES greed, ego, and even a dash of artistic integrity into those seemingly innocuous lists of names at the beginning and end of every film. Called credits, the concept has been around since the days when painters first started signing their works and writers put their names beneath the titles of their manuscripts. In film, however, the element of collaboration has turned a simple process into one that often requires intense negotiation, lengthy contracts, and considerable ingenuity.

Credit squabbles involving stars seem to concern primarily ego, not money. The placement of an actor's name on a film involves two factors, size and order. The actor's agent and the producer must come to an agreement that stipulates how big the actor's name will be in comparison with the title (same size? 75 percent? 50 percent?) and whether the actor's name will appear above or below the title and the names of any other actors. These negotiations are carried on independently of salary negotiations.

Occasionally, two superstars will grace the same film, underscoring the difficulty of designing credits that are *exactly* equal. The basic problem here is that people read from top to bottom and from left to right, so that whoever has his name on top or to the left appears to be first billed. In the film *The Towering Inferno* Paul Newman and Steve McQueen were both top-billed, equally, above the title. This was accomplished by putting Newman's name above McQueen's but McQueen's name to the left of Newman's. Naturally both names were in the same size type.

The film *Staircase* had a similar situation with its leads, Richard Burton and Rex Harrison, and an even more creative solution. The two names were printed over and over again on alternating steps of a staircase. The camera zoomed into the steps while quickly traveling down them, so that it was impossible to tell which name had appeared first.

Credits mean money as well as ego fulfillment. For some, like writers, salary frequently depends on their credit. For others, payment is secure, but the credit could mean more or better-paying jobs in the future, especially if the film turns out to be a hit.

When the movies began, credits were all but nonexistent. Even the actors went unidentified. Gradually producers began to give credit to more and more of the people who made the movies, a trend that has continued to this day, with production secretaries, accountants, and caterers now receiving credit on some of the bigger films.

The classic approach to credits is to have all the credits at the beginning of the film, starting with the stars, then the title, then the rest of the actors; following them would be the technical credits and, finally, the credits for writing, producing, and directing. At the end of the film the names of the entire cast would be reprised, this time on a list telling who played which character.

A more modern approach features just the names of the major stars at the beginning, along with writer, producer, and director, followed by a few of the most prominent technical credits, such as cinematography, editing, and music. At the end are all the other credits, rolling up the screen as the customers make their way to the exits. This approach is especially suited to big productions, since it allows the film to begin without forcing the viewers to do three or four minutes' worth of reading.

Within limits it is the producers who assign the credits. These limits include contractual obligations to actors, guild rules, and, in the case of screenwriters, a Writers Guild arbitration process. The one area where there are no rules is producer's credits.

Most of the time, the first thing to appear on the screen is the logo of a studio. It is there because the studio is distributing the film. It may also be there because the studio has bankrolled the film as well, although studio coproductions are becoming common. In the case of a coproduction, one company usually distributes in the United States while the other takes the rest of the world. Which logo would appear would depend on where you saw the film. Even little-known distribution companies now attach their logos to the beginning of their films.

The distributor's logo is a time-honored tradition, but what comes next can be just about anything. It may be the names of one, two, or even three stars; it may be the name of an executive producer (that is, "so-and-so presents," or "a so-and-so production"), or it may even be the name of a production company. Whatever it is, it is usually arranged by contract long before the film goes into production.

A production company could very easily be just what its name implies: a producer with sharp entrepreneurial instincts melding a handful of outside investors into a unit capable of financing a film made completely outside of the studio system. After completion a deal (called a pickup) might be struck that would call for the studio to distribute, either by buying the film outright or by sharing the profits.

Often, the owner of the production company is also listed as executive producer. He may "present" the film as well. To be in such a position, at least one of the following three things is usually required: owning a literary property, being a major star, or having control of enough money to finance the film. The simplest example would be tiny Malpaso Productions, Clint Eastwood's company. Since Eastwood is a sought-after star, the other two ingredients needed to get a film off the ground—a literary property and financing—both gravitate toward him. A studio that wants Eastwood's services will first give Eastwood the money to buy a screenplay or have one written. Then the studio will give Eastwood the financing to make his film and the assurance that it won't be looking over his shoulder. Since Eastwood and his company (just one or two other individuals) decide which movie to make and spend the money as they see fit, it's legitimate to see the Malpaso name on his films. It would also be legitimate to see Eastwood's name listed as producer or executive producer, but he tends to decline those credits.

Sometimes, the executive producer credit will go to someone who had only one of the three ingredients. Bernie Brillstein was an executive producer of *The Blues Brothers* because as the manager of John Belushi and Dan Aykroyd, he provided the stars. Likewise Jay Bernstein was an executive producer of *Sunburn* because he was Farrah Fawcett's manager at the time. "I didn't really have anything to do," Bernstein later noted, adding that his "labor" netted him $50,000.

On that same film, *Sunburn*, there was a credit that read, "A Tuesday Films Production in association with Philip Waxman." By all accounts, Tuesday Films was one of those production companies set up to minimize legal liabilities, and also for tax purposes. Waxman, a veteran producer, had his name (without any sort of title) on the film because he had brought the literary property to the attention of the production company that eventually made it. Not being an agent, Waxman was forbidden by law to take a 10-percent cut of the sale. Instead, he got a flat fee and his name on the screen.

Finally, someone who is just a moneyman may be listed as executive producer. Mel Simon falls into this category, but in his case the presence of large sums of his money tends to attract scripts and literary properties to his large, independent production company. A more classic example might be one Walter Fiveson, executive producer of a low-budget film called *The Clonus Horror* and also head of the Polyglycoat Corporation. Fiveson had only two involvements with that film: He put up most of the money for it, and he was the father of the director, Robert Fiveson.

A little less nebulous than the duties of executive producer are those of the producer.* In most cases it is the producer who stands at the intersection of money and creativity. He decides which talent to hire —actors, writers, directors, some of the crew—and he also makes such decisions as where and when to shoot the film. He is, as well, de facto story editor (along with the director) and can order rewrites or hire new writers. If the executive producer delivers the major elements, the producer forges those elements into a movie, overcoming thousands of logistical hurdles, great and small.

Even though he is often an employee himself, the producer is, in effect, the boss of the film. On his (or her) shoulders is the responsibility for overcoming the inertia that tends to block the progress of every project—and also the blame if there is failure. He also has the final control of how the budget will be spent.

Although there's rarely a listing of such in the credits, most producers are known in the industry as line producers. They act as overseers, shepherding the film through production, making the hard decisions about the compromises that have to be made when things go wrong. They also mediate arguments, especially those that arise between stars and directors, since there is no set hierarchy on those rarefied levels.

Once the film is completed, the producer's duties are still not over. On independent films he is responsible for securing distribution deals; on studio productions he is relieved of that burden but is still obligated to give an accounting to all those in line to share in the film's profits. He usually receives two forms of compensation: a producer's fee (which can be as high as $50,000 in the low-budget range and can soar to a quarter of a million on big productions) and a piece of the profits. A typical movie deal splits the profits evenly between the producer and the investors. Out of the producer's share of the profits must then come whatever percentages have been promised to the talent (although some stars get a percentage of the gross receipts). Whatever is left over belongs to the producer.

Helping the producer handle logistical problems is someone called

*Exceptions abound, however. On the film *Bronco Billy*, for example, the two writers were given producer's credits, while Eastwood himself acted as the real—and uncredited —producer.

an associate producer. Although this could very easily be a post given to someone's brother-in-law, it is more likely a position for a producer-in-training. Basically, the job requires coordinating the details of the outside services film crews use, as well as overall troubleshooting on the set.

Just about now in our hypothetical example there would be the writer's credit. The ideal situation, from almost everyone's point of view, is for there to be one writer, who conceived the story out of the blue and wrote every draft of the screenplay. It rarely happens.

More often, several writers will work on a script, one after the other. If the script is based on a novel, a credit will say that. But if the idea originated in screenplay form, things get a little more complicated. Often, the person who wrote the original draft of the screenplay will be credited with "story by," or "original story by." That's because his draft is almost never used. At least one writer rewrites it and, sometimes, as many as a dozen.

When there are legions of writers involved or, for that matter, any number greater than one, the Writers Guild usually determines who gets which credit—an act that in turn determines the money each will be paid. Some of the writer's income is, of course, independent of credit; he's hired to do a job and gets paid for it. Credit, however, establishes how much money he'll get in the event of a sale of the film to television, and whether he'll own the rights to the property in other media (for example, novelizations).

At least half of all major productions go to Writers Guild arbitration. The stakes can be as high as $100,000 for a TV payment, and that residual has to be divided equally among the number of writers receiving the "screenplay by" credit. (But not the "story by" credit. *Those* writers have the right to sell the novelization and certain other subsidiary items—which could also go for hundreds of thousands.)

Judging which writers did what falls to other writers in a quick and reasonably fair arbitration process. The writers read all the different drafts and try to assign credits. Usually, the first writer on a project gets the story credit and the last the screenplay credit. The arbiters also try to assign no more than two or three names to each category, for a total of four or five credited writers. Why not give credit to all the writers, as they do with actors (and as is often done for writers of foreign films)? According to a Writers Guild spokesman, "That would demean the writing credit." In other words, it's perfectly acceptable to go through writers as one would pairs of socks, but the public needn't be confronted with this information.

The last of the major, front-of-the-film credits is director. He is the one who interprets the script, gives the dialogue nuance, and maintains the artistic balance of the story. Increasingly, he also has considerable input into what that story will be. Usually, the contribution of the director is recognized by the credit "A [director's name] film."

On the most basic level the director does one thing: He chooses the camera angles from which the story will be filmed. Will there be one long static shot, or will there be lots of cuts from close-up to close-up, or will the camera move all around the action? These are director's decisions. He must also decide how the action will flow—from left to right, up or down, back and forth—in what is called "blocking" the actors, or telling them which movements to make.

The next level of directorial competence is in judging performances. But judging them isn't enough; a good director knows how to draw good performances from the actors. Part psychologist, part visual stylist, and part storyteller, the director has the most challenging (and most envied) job on the set.

Once the film is over, the closing credits usually crawl up the screen. These are mainly technical credits, but the major ones do involve a good deal of artistic input.

Music is a challenge within a challenge: Not only must the composer invent rhythms and melodies that sound good, he must also squeeze them or extend them to fit time requirements that have been clocked to the second. Adding to the headaches is time pressure of a different sort: The composer cannot even begin his work until the images have been completely assembled. Often, this very difficult job is sandwiched into a few weeks, during which the composer not only creates the music but may arrange it and conduct it as well. Occasionally assisting composers are music editors, who position the recorded music on the film's soundtrack.

It's a running joke in Hollywood that if a film does not do well, and no reason for its failure is apparent, then it was the fault of the music. On the other hand, music can certainly add an entirely new dimension to an otherwise indifferent offering, as John Williams's heroic score did for *Superman.*

Composers receive three types of compensations: fees, residuals, and, if they are as prominent as Williams, a share of the profits.

Another prominent technical credit is *editor.* He (or very often she) is the one who assembles the pieces of picture and dialogue into a coherent whole. Even if he chooses to do this by following the script to the letter, he may still impose his own ideas on a scene by determining what is shown during that scene: Will it be, for example, the person speaking or the person listening? Very subtly, the editor can choose to make a protagonist out of a minor character or, just as easily, turn a hero into a supporting character—and that's without altering the script. However, since the editor *can* alter the script, he could make the movie something that doesn't even remotely resemble the original story—that's how much power the editor has, for good or for ill. Practicalities, such as the fact that he is an employee of the producer, mean that the editor cannot act totally on his own. Increasingly the director as well supervises the editor, although the director, in turn, may be overruled by the production company.

Film editing requires the kind of analytical intelligence that enables a person always to keep in mind the overview—the film as a whole—while making very detailed decisions about the most trivial matters, such as the exact instant to begin or end a scene. Sometimes an editor attends the shooting of the film to advise the director on the camera angles and the blocking of the actors, but his real work is done after the shooting in a tiny editing room. Often, he is aided by one or two assistants, who catalogue bits of film for him, and a sound editor, who attends to the mammoth job of positioning every sound effect on the film's sound track.

The final major "techno-artistic" credit is for the *director of photography (D.P.)*. His main function is lighting the subject matter—no small contribution in the eyes of anyone who is aware that motion picture lighting is a good deal more complicated than just hitting the subject with a couple of floodlights. But many people—even in Hollywood—are not aware of this. Cinematographers are often commended for their brillance on the basis of spectacular scenery they have shot, when in reality the credit should go to the director for choosing that subject and to nature for creating it.

From the late silent era to the early 1950s, cinematography involved a lot more artifice than is now the fashion, especially in black and white. Shadows were heightened and distorted for effect; close-ups were often high-quality glamour photographs that moved. Today lighting tends to call very little attention to itself, but this too presents a challenge, since it is not easy to achieve a level of visual consistency that makes people forget they're looking at a film.

To achieve this end, the D.P. uses various kinds of artificial lights. Outdoors, he uses powerful carbon arc lights, often in combination with shiny metallic boards, called reflectors, which are used to fill in the shadows.

Among the crew the D.P. is one of the most respected positions, with managerial as well as artistic responsibilities. He is the foreman of the camera crew and has, in theory, risen from the ranks of assistant cameramen and camera operators.

Right below the D.P. is the *camera operator,* who sits at the camera, peering through the viewfinder. In addition to a keen eye the operator also needs considerable dexterity in order to follow motion with the camera. The director relies on the operator to make sure that what has been photographed is exactly what the director wanted.

In European credits you might see a "focus puller" credit and a "clapper/loader" credit. These refer to first and second assistant cameramen. One adjusts focus on the camera lens, sometimes while the camera is running (the camera operator is too busy shooting to do that), while the other, the clapper/loader, loads film into the camera and claps the slate, that familiar small blackboard with a stick that is whacked before the director yells, "Action." The clap sound is necessary because picture and sound are initially on two separate pieces of stock—film for the picture and tape for the sound. The sound of the sticks hitting and the picture of it provide a reference for synchronizing the two. One of the assistant cameramen, usually the one who claps the slate, also keeps a record of each shot on each roll of film. When a roll is completed, it is developed into a negative, and prints are made from that. Thanks to the camera reports, only a few sections of each roll—the good takes—have to be printed. That saves a lot of money. Numbers and letters on the slate identify each shot.

The *gaffer* is also under the leadership of the director of photography. Once the D.P. decides what lights are needed and where they should be placed, the gaffer sets them up. (The word *gaffer* is sometimes applied to anyone who rigs anything, such as stunt gaffer.) The gaffer has an assistant, a *best boy,* who is mainly concerned with the electrical wiring of the lights. He keeps the cords from becoming an indecipherable mass of black spaghetti.

An *electrician* makes sure there is power for those lights. He is custodian of the sound stage's power lines, or if filming on location, he maintains the gasoline-powered generators that provide electricity to the company.

A parallel to the camera crew is the *sound crew,* although these workers have considerably less status, since picture is irreplaceable, whereas any sound that has been recorded can usually be duplicated later in a recording studio. As a result of this thinking, the visual element always comes first; seldom will the composition of a shot be compromised just to accommodate the presence of a microphone. If it's a choice between good sound and good picture, the sound usually loses.

The head of the sound department, the *sound recordist* or *mixer,* is always on the set, running the tape recorder that records the sound of every scene. He supervises the work of a *boom operator,* who maneuvers a long mechanical arm, or boom, designed to allow a microphone to dangle over a group of actors. When the confines of the set make the use of a boom impractical, the boom operator will simply hold the microphone off-camera, aiming at the subject. With luck the boom operator will graduate into a recordist job.

Rerecording mixers work in recording studios and meld the finished sound tracks—dialogue, music, sound effects—into a single track; or two, for stereo, or four, or five, or whatever is called for. The mixers never see the actual shooting, but they do work with the actors. Much of the sound that's so carefully recorded during filming, especially on location, just isn't good enough for the high-quality sound tracks we have come to expect from movies. So when the shooting is over, the actors usually have to spend a week or two in a dark dubbing studio, saying their lines again, trying to match their words to the lip movements they see projected on a screen before them—all in the hope that this new recording will have better quality sound.

After the camera and sound crews, the rest of the company is roughly divided into four more branches: the preproduction group, the individual specialists, the director's crew, and the producer's group.

THE PREPRODUCTION GROUP

The preproduction people help decide who and what to film. *Casting* is a function that used to be handled almost exclusively by the studios. Today, there are independent casting consultants who are hired by producers on a film-to-film basis. Their job is to match actors to scripts, and all of their suggestions need to be approved by the producer and director. The one group for which the casting directors are not responsible are the stars. These are usually cast by the producers.

The *art director* helps select and/or create the look of the sets and locations. With period pieces and science fiction films this is no small job, but usually even with films that require a documentary look the art director must still find appropriate locations.

When his chores are expanded to include bringing a sense of coherent style to props and costumes as well as sets and, perhaps, special effects, the art director will often get a credit as *production designer.*

Working with art directors and production designers are *set designers,* whose architectural and engineering skills help them actualize the art director's ideas. The construction work itself is done by a small corps of studio *carpenters, painters,* and *plumbers.*

Working with the art director—but assigned to the production during shooting—is a *set decorator,* who attends to the small, movable objects on the set: paintings on the wall, bookshelves, record racks, table settings, and so on.

The *costume designer* either designs or selects clothing for the cast and, as such, is essentially a preproduction employee. During shooting, *wardrobe masters* and *wardrobe mistresses* attend to the costumes of the actors and actresses, respectively. They repair any damage and make sure the costumes are not lost, and that they look the same from shot to shot.

The *prop man,* or *property master,* either obtains or makes special items called for by the script. The item can be as simple as a pistol or a wristwatch or as complicated as a mechanical shark. Prop men (and, increasingly often, independent specialists) make and then attend the shooting to maintain these props. They are the custodians of all the props.

THE INDIVIDUAL SPECIALISTS

The on-the-set specialists include a *greensman,* who is essentially a gardener as well as a sort of prop man who deals exclusively with plants. There's also a *wrangler,* who handles animals, although in the case of animals that do special tricks, there will usually be an *animal trainer* credited.

Makeup and *hairdressing* are obvious credits, but not so obvious is the fact that these crewmen put in some of the longest hours on the set. They have to arrive every morning long before shooting starts to make up the actors; then they must stay until the last shot each day, making sure that hair and makeup are just right. If not, they do touch-ups. Finally, they must bring a sense of continuity to their jobs, making sure, for example, that the hair will always be parted on the same side or that the lipstick will always be the same shade.

The *grips* are the handymen of the set. Their most frequent responsibility is to move things around to prepare for each new camera setup (what they can and cannot move is designated by union rules), but they also help arrange difficult camera emplacements by building scaffolds or by setting up tracks that the camera dolly can move along during complicated shots. Mechanical ingenuity and a strong back are the hallmarks of successful grips.

Drivers are not the people who stage car chases. They are, instead, employees whose main duty is to transport cast and crew to and from locations. They may do some errands during the day, but just as often they will play cards or sleep.

Stuntmen, and *stuntwomen,* thanks in part to Burt Reynolds's romantic depiction of them in *Hooper,* have been elevated to the role of contemporary hero. They fall, fight, perform driving stunts and anything else called for by the script. They are usually paid by the stunt, and stunts are often bid by a number of stuntmen. One leap from a pier costs perhaps $500, whether or not the take is used. Sometimes, as with fire stunts, the stuntman will do the job on the proviso that it be done once only, no matter what. Stuntmen are not full-time employees of the studios; they have their own organizations, which often contract to do all the stunts for a given film. *Stunt coordinators* have a job that constitutes happy old age for stuntmen. They plan the stunts with the director and watch in comfort while their younger colleagues—often sons or grandsons—take the chances they once took.

Special effects is a title that's being seen more and more in the *Star Wars* era. It encompasses everything from making models to computer animation. Sometimes it even includes rigging certain kinds of stunts. As with so many other specialties, effects people used to work for the studios, but now the trend is toward independent companies. With their own equipment—including shooting stages or computers—they can supply producers with complete footage of earthquakes, space wars, avalanches, or explosions. One soundman told us a good way to discover whether or not an effects specialist was any good: "If he's over thirty-five and has all his fingers, he knows what he's doing."

The *unit publicist* usually tries to draw media coverage to the film while it is being shot. On-the-set interviews with stars and director for newspapers, TV, and magazines are the goal, so that the film becomes known as early as possible. But there's a hidden agenda here, too. The publicist knows that all that free media coverage has much less effect on attendance than the concerted ad campaign that will be mounted when the film comes out; so the goal of publicity during production is not so much to influence the general public as it is to influence the theater owners, who are especially attuned to this sort of advance coverage. If the film looks good to them at this point, it will be easier for the distributor to get the theater owners to play the film.

The journalists, who seem to be unaware that they are being used in this way, are invited to the studios or out to the locations (often at the studio or production company's expense) and allowed to stay there for a while, gathering information. To assure that the show business press will come when beckoned, the hot interview subjects make it a point of being available to reporters at this time, and this time only. If a newspaper editor wants an interview with Jane Fonda or Robert Redford, he's almost forced to do it in connection with her or his current film.

Working with the publicist is a *still photographer*, whose on-the-set photos will eventually appear in newspapers and magazines, accompanying interviews and, later, reviews. Once upon a time these stills were also used in the display cases of theaters, but this is increasingly less common.

THE DIRECTOR'S CREW

In a sense, everyone in the crew works to support the director, but more practically speaking, the director has a small corps of personnel who work most closely with him. The closest—in physical terms, anyway—is the *script supervisor*, or *continuity person*, who is often literally at the director's elbow. This person, often a woman, keeps track of everything that has gone on film: which scenes, what has been said, what the camera angles were, the positions of the actors and the props, and even what the weather conditions were. Polaroid pictures are a big help in keeping it all straight.

The script supervisor jots notes on her copy of the script, indicating which shot contained which actions and which dialogue; every shot has a different number. She also notes the positioning of the actors within the scenes and what they are doing, so that in following scenes the actions will match. It would be impossible to splice two shots together if one of them had an actor lighting a cigarette with his left hand and the other had him lighting it with his right. When the shooting is finished, the script supervisor's script goes to the editor.

Working closely with the script supervisor is a *dialogue coach,* who works on the occasional scene when only one participant in a conversation is seen on camera. The dialogue coach sometimes reads the part of the unseen actor, so that the actor who is being photographed has something to respond to. The coach may also feed lines to forgetful actors, although this is usually done by the script supervisor.

The job of *assistant director* less often leads to directing than it does to producing. The concerns of this particular job are production oriented rather than aesthetic: maintaining discipline among the crew and keeping tabs on the actors, making sure they are available when needed.

Another duty is crowd control over the extras. Although crowd scenes usually look frenzied and disorganized, they are, in fact, carefully choreographed by the A.D.'s. If the story is of epic proportions, there will be several assistant directors.

Occasionally, there will be a credit for *"Directors Guild trainee,"* an assistant to the assistant director. To counter charges of nepotism, racism, and sexism in motion picture industry hiring practices, the Directors Guild of America (DGA) sponsors open testing for this position. The written tests are general aptitude and intelligence tests, with many multiple choice questions. Those who pass these first tests are then interviewed by a DGA panel. It's during the interviews— which are far more subjective than the written tests—that the DGA panel members have the latitude to broaden the racial and sexual mix of their guild.

The *second unit director* may never meet the director. He is involved with the shooting of stunts, some crowd scenes (such as battles), and special effects—elements that are filmed apart in time and place from the principal photography. Often a former stuntman, the second unit director commands his own small crew and choreographs all the action to be filmed as well as selecting the angles from which it will be shot. The only thing he doesn't usually do is shoot scenes with dialogue.

THE PRODUCER'S GROUP

The final segment of the company might be considered the producer's group. These are people who deal with the logistics and practicalities of getting the film made—on time and for the alloted budget.

The first duty of the *production manager,* or *unit manager,* involves a preproduction breakdown of the script so that the story can be shot as economically as possible. In scheduling the order of the shooting the manager takes into account such things as availability of actors and locations, sets, props, and weather. The end result, with luck, is a schedule that allows all the filming on a particular location to be done at one time so the company will not have to keep moving back and forth. In the same way, the actors' time is utilized carefully, although for obvious reasons this sort of scheduling involves considerable compromise.

During shooting, the unit manager handles the company's business, selecting the widely varying outside companies that supply goods and services to the crew and, when necessary, arranging for housing for the cast and crew. He can also hire additional laborers when necessary.

Helping the unit manager is the *production accountant,* who keeps track of all the expenditures, and a *production secretary,* who is usually based in the company's office and is the cast and crew's link with the outside world, since many shooting locations don't have phones. The secretary naturally attends to whatever secretarial work is required by the production, and during the period of shooting, such chores, as well as the inevitable "go-fering," can take up to fourteen or fifteen hours a day. Also involved are *production assistants,* whose jobs often mean leaving the set to perform various errands.

Production executives are studio employees, often at the vice-presidential level, who oversee the production from the studio's end. This executive is the liaison between the studio and the production and might also be the individual who discovered the script or perhaps served as the matchmaker among script, producer, and director.

Since even some of the studios now describe themselves as banks for filmmakers, the production executive might be considered a loan officer (although the financial arrangements are actually investments, not loans). Like a loan officer, however, the production executive must evaluate how well the studio's money has been spent during production and, if necessary, recommend (or not recommend) additional funding to the head of production.

The remaining credits are essentially acknowledgments of suppliers: the lab, the cameras, the lenses, and other miscellany. There are trade-outs, too, as when a company gets free use of vehicles and then thanks the automobile company on screen for providing them, or when the company shoots on certain locations and gives a "grateful acknowledgment" to the owner.

There you have it—scores of workers, each doing compartmentalized jobs that eventually unite in a finished film. But as the Russ Meyer model in the next chapter proves, this whole structure is far from being a necessity. Union crews are criticized for being unnecessarily large, inefficient, and overpaid. On small features these are valid considerations, but on large features, because of the logistics, and on TV series, because of the time element, the crews are a real asset. How else could forty-eight minutes of presentable film for TV be shot in just six to ten days? A small, nonunion crew would take about twenty-four days to do the same. As for the question of pay, union wage scales have always taken into account the seasonal periods of unemployment faced by the crewmen.

Crew work, especially on the union side, is blue collar work, done by blue collar workers. Don't expect to meet many film school aesthetes on a union crew. As in many other businesses, union membership is a father-to-son thing, with a single family producing generations of prop men or makeup men. Like the English class system, there's little room for upward (or even sideways) mobility. So, there isn't much fraternization with cast and executive echelons. Union rules don't forbid it, but the differences in life-style, economic circumstance, and education effectively separate those who wear Guccis and sports coats from those who wear Addidas and down-filled vests.

2

THE COMPONENTS:

RUSS MEYER

RUSS MEYER HAS BEEN PRAISED BY SOME AND CONDEMNED BY OTHERS, but he deserves inclusion in an introduction to how things work in the movie business for two reasons: The way he makes movies offers a clear example of some of the important components of picture making. And, Meyer has been phenomenally successful. His films rarely cost over $250,000 or take more than eight weeks to shoot. But they rarely bomb, either. His track record of thirty hits, marred by a scant two flops, has made the "T & A tycoon" the subject of talk shows, documentaries, and even an article in *Forbes*, the business magazine.

Meyer's one-man mode, it must be remembered, is distinctly atypical of the way things are done in the movie business. But the elements he deals with are the same that all executive producers deal with, whether they are making *Beneath the Valley of the Ultravixens* or *The Empire Strikes Back*. Among them are the following:

The Story

In Hollywood, photocopying stores regularly advertise scripts as one of their specialties. Typists make a living at home doing nothing but typing scripts and story outlines. Secretarial services specialize in editing, typing, and mimeographing screenplays. Hundreds of agents peddle their clients' writing, while some 8,000 scripts are registered with the Writers Guild every year—more than 650 scripts a month.

Entire divisions, story departments, exist at studios to sort through some of this material. Yet with all that volume around, Meyer relies mostly on himself, a combination of wanting to be a true auteur and being unable to pay the sometimes astronomical amounts that are asked for good scripts. A few people do submit scripts to him anyway. Meyer usually reads them and rejects them.

Meyer's ideas originate in his fantasy life, which centers on women with gargantuan breasts and, to a lesser extent, on outrageous violence and sadism. Sometimes Meyer spends a few weeks writing a detailed shooting script, but at other times he has hired a collaborator, most often the Pulitzer Prize–winning movie critic for the Chicago *Sun-Times*, Roger Ebert.

Like everyone else's movies, Meyer's are first expressed verbally, often as little more than a few scenes and a handful of characters in search of a plot and unifying theme. With luck, these ingredients come later. After bouncing his ideas off friends and associates, Meyer goes to work on a treatment or outline, which is basically the film in short-story form.

Although a Meyer script can go through as many steps and revisions as a script for a studio production, there's a significant difference: At the studio, the changes are made in order to please as many as a score of people (for example, the stars, the studio executives, the producer, the director), each of whom judges the script from a separate perspective. When Meyer rewrites his scripts, he does it only to satisfy himself.

The Financing

Traditional wisdom in Hollywood says that the story comes first; without it there would be no film. We beg to differ. Often, it's a case of the money having already been raised, with the producers looking around frantically for an appropriate story. In Meyer's case, both story and money are nurtured together, and to some degree they both come from Meyer himself.

Thanks to a couple of immensely successful films in the late 1960s, Meyer was a millionaire by 1970. With his films costing less than $100,000 in those preinflationary days, he could finance them entirely out of his own pocket—which he did not always choose to do. Usually, he would have three sources of financing available to him, and often on a film, he would combine all three. Besides his personal fortune, there was also money from the film company of which he was president but not sole owner. This company made money through the distribution of old Meyer films—films that seem immune to obsolescence.

The third source of financing continues to be outside investors. Often these are friends of Meyer's from his army days, or business associates, such as small, regional film distributors. No single investor puts up a majority of the money, and none has control over the enterprise. In exchange for use of their money, the investors get their investment returned out of the proceeds of the movie and then a percentage of the profits. (It's important to note that Meyer takes these percentages very seriously, unlike many producers. Mario Puzo, for example, once recalled that he had been given 10 percent of the producer's net on the first *Godfather* movie but had never seen a cent, due mainly to Paramount's having written off numerous unexpected expenses to the film. In contrast, 10 percent of the producer's net on Meyer's 1975 film *The Supervixens* would have eventually yielded more than $50,000.)

Preproduction

Studios have entire departments for budgeting, casting, set design and construction, props, costuming, and location scouting; individual companies exist to provide those services to independent producers. Meyer does it all himself.

He will go out in his own four-wheel-drive vehicle to find just the right mountain. He will help hammer in the nails that hold his sets together. He and an associate will work out the budget and then administer it. He will personally cast the film out of the Motion Picture Academy's guide to Screen Actors Guild members, and he will go to the store to buy costumes for them.

Interestingly, on what are otherwise rock-bottom enterprises, the cast is all union, except for a handful of walk-ons. Although Meyer does not use union crews, he does go with the Screen Actors Guild, because, he says, the Guild imposes a level of professionalism on his actors that makes Meyer believe that their steep minimum salary is almost a bargain ($1,000 a week in 1980).

Meyer uses Guild unknowns for one reason: They'll work for this minimum. But when someone who has been driving a truck to subsist suddenly becomes the male lead of a feature film, temperament and ego often become major problems. Guild rules, which demand and enforce stringent standards, seem to be a formidable antidote.

As for the female leads, many of them are strippers, with only a casual interest in acting until Meyer offers to pluck them out of obscurity. Though he is a loudly proclaimed, active heterosexual, Meyer is not a "casting couch" producer—no more than anyone else, anyway. Because he sees so few women he likes (in the area of figure only—acting is almost irrelevant), Meyer finds himself not in a position to make any extracurricular demands on his potential actresses. That's not to say that he doesn't sleep with his leading ladies; he just doesn't demand it as a prerequisite of working for him.

For the women, a chance to work in a Meyer film is an opportunity to get a much-sought-after Guild membership card and something even more sought after: the chance to show an agent or producer what she looks like on celluloid. With depressing regularity, however, women who appear in Meyer films seldom make it as actresses. It's generally (and sometimes incorrectly) assumed that they are stigmatized by appearing in X-rated material (a situation that often rules out potentially lucrative work in commercials) or that they are not dedicated professionals.

All of Meyer's preproduction work is done out of a few small rooms: an office near Hollywood Boulevard, a high-rise apartment, or a home in the Hollywood Hills. Often, Meyer sleeps in the next room, either turning his office into a home or his home into an office. And, equally frequently, he will use those rooms as a location for part of his movie.

Because the Meyer method is so removed from the studio prepro-duction model, it's tempting to dismiss his work as being little more than home movies. Yet these "home movies" compete with Hollywood films at multiple theaters throughout the world—and you pay the same amount to see one as you do the other.

Production

Since it's physically impossible to run a camera and sound equipment at the same time, Meyer has to rely on other people to help him film his movies. Again, it's a bare essentials situation. The crew rarely exceeds eight people. With union crews the division of labor is legend-ary; it's often been called featherbedding. Sound people can't even touch props, camera people can't touch light cables, and so on and so forth. On a Meyer set everybody usually pitches in and does whatever needs to be done. Of no one is this more true than Meyer himself, whose "official" jobs are producer, director, cinematographer, and camera operator. Unofficially, Meyer is a grip as well, and, as the chief enforcer of cast and crew discipline, he might be said to be his own assistant director, too.

Meyer is the first to acknowledge that his crew approach could never hope to cope with the logistics of a high-budget movie. Crowd scenes, musical numbers, and *Star Wars* special effects are all out of the question, not just because of their expense but also because it would be just too much work for eight people. Even so, Meyer films have featured car chases, brawls, and massive explosions.

Also out of the question are complicated, convoluted shots involving lots of camera movement. These, too, require large crews to accom-plish and are therefore beyond Meyer. Meyer's response to these limitations has been to use a "lock-down" style, in which the camera seldom pans or trucks or moves in any way during the shot. To compen-sate for the stasis inherent in such shooting, Meyer breaks each scene into many more individual shots than another director would.

Paradoxically, this style creates still more work for the crew. Instead of taking just one shot—or setup—of two people talking, Meyer will invariably reshoot the scene over and over again, from every conceivable angle. Each new angle requires camera, lights, and other equipment to be repositioned. Studio productions cover scenes this way, too, but they have scores of workmen to move all that equipment quickly. Incredibly, a Meyer crew achieves just as many setups, or more, per day, usually because the shots he chooses are relatively simple. Moreover, he takes about as many weeks—eight to twelve—to film his features as do the studios, although Meyer continues to reshoot small, undemanding scenes well into the postproduction phase.

With a handful of people making a movie along the same time schedule that major features are made, there's got to be a lot of hard work, and no one puts forth more of that than Meyer himself. Still, partly because Meyer often hires novices, he is a harsh taskmaster.

While twelve-hour workdays are a standard feature of film production, Meyer's casts and crews are subjected to additional toil, because each is doing several jobs, including the actors on occasion. Supervising all this labor is Meyer himself, who's been known to fly into a screaming rage when he feels someone is not doing his share. Meyer defends himself by pointing out that sometimes such "motivation" is required in order to get the film completed. Often, though, he's talked about his own workaholic nature, and a companion superstition that seems to be that the film will only be a winner if everyone—especially Meyer —is worked to a state of near exhaustion. This philosophy has made Meyer a lot of enemies among the ranks of his former actors and employees.

Also contributing to Meyer's lack of popularity are certain off-hours policies. Generally speaking, a five-day-a-week, twelve-hour-a-day work schedule, beginning every day at six or seven A.M., leaves little time for a social life, except perhaps on the weekends. Actors are even more hard pressed because they usually spend their time off learning their dialogue. During shooting on distant locations (far enough from Hollywood to make a hotel necessary), filming goes on six full days a week. So, with all this in mind, it might be assumed that Meyer wouldn't begrudge cast or crew a little recreation; but he does.

First, it's reasonable for a producer to want his leading man not to show up with a hangover every morning. To avoid this, Meyer and one or two associates (usually old army buddies) will keep off-hours tabs on the entire company. Ideally for Meyer, everyone will be billeted in a single isolated motel or lodge. Second, and quite incredibly, in view of the kind of films he makes, Meyer encourages celibacy among cast and crew.

He prefers actresses who don't have a lover/manager, as so many of them do, for these men, Meyer has said, often start making unreasonable demands. He has occasionally enforced a rule about co-workers not having sex with one another, and by isolating his employees so effectively when on location, he makes extracurricular involvement difficult. He even frowns on visits by mates, for he considers them distracting. It all boils down to a military approach—intolerable in big-budget productions but, in all likelihood, the only way a small independent can turn out a competitive product.

Postproduction

The postproduction phase of filmmaking includes editing, most of the sound work, the music, and all the lab work. It might be assumed that the studios have it all over Meyer in these areas, but that's not the case.

Just as Meyer rents cameras and props from small independent suppliers and hires friends (and friends of friends) to fill out his crews, he is at no disadvantage because he is nonunion and not affiliated with a studio. Everything he, or any other filmmaker, needs is either rentable or buyable.

The first step of postproduction actually begins on the first day of shooting. This involves engaging a film lab to develop the negative that has been shot that day and make positive prints from it. In studio production this is the camera department's responsibility, and they will go to whatever lab is owned by the studio. Most of these same labs, however, welcome the chance to deal with independents, so people such as Meyer can pick and choose.

Since editing is basically a months-long wedding of human and Moviola, only a small room is needed for the coupling. Meyer will either rent such a room or bring an editing machine into his home, where he will personally edit. He'll also bring a sound transfer machine to his house. The machine transfers dialogue and sound effects from the recording tape that was used during shooting to magnetic film stock.

Additional sound work consists of dubbing (recording dialogue to fit actors' lip movements whenever the originally recorded material isn't up to par) and folleying (doing the same with sound effects). Special sound stages can be rented for this purpose, but Meyer often uses his home to do the job.

The music is invariably contracted out to a composer, who watches the film on the Moviola and then writes and arranges a score. The composer then hires musicians and a recording hall for them to perform in.

The next-to-last step in postproduction is called mixing, in which all the different kinds of sound are blended onto a single track. This procedure requires a small theater and a lot of bulky, expensive equipment. It also requires a couple of highly paid technicians. Studios have all these resources right on their lots, but Meyer has to go out and rent them. It is a special burden to him because his sound is more complicated (which means more time consuming and more expensive) than most other low-budget productions. Meyer has been known to lay off some of these costs by cutting the sound company's owner in on a small piece of the film's profits.

Once the sound is finished, the negative is cut to conform to the work print, and after a few intermediate steps, release prints are made by the lab. These rolls of film are what will be projected in the theaters.

Meyer will usually have between 75 and 125 prints made—no small investment at about $1,000 per print. (It should be noted, however, that Meyer's purchase of prints is through his function as distributor, not producer.)

Distribution

In the sense of getting a lot of people to go see a movie, studio distribution is clearly superior to Meyer's approach. It has to be, with thousands of people working worldwide to bring in the mass audience. In the sense of a filmmaker using distribution to make money for himself, however, the Meyer approach beats the studio system hands down.

Before we elaborate on Meyer's distribution, it should be pointed out that there is no division into separate camps: Studios often make deals to distribute independently made films. But in Meyer's case, the studios would be leery because of the X-rated content. Meyer would be leery, too, because he knows he would stand a much smaller chance of seeing any earnings. Traditionally it has not been the theater owner who makes money on movies, nor has it been the producer; it has always been the distributor.

But because of the complicated logistics involved in setting up an effective distribution company, even the most rebellious independent producers shy away from self-distribution. Not Russ Meyer, though.

Meyer personally distributes almost all his thirty-odd films. In addition to paying for prints and advertising, he must also occasionally make deals with individual theaters and arrange subdistribution contracts with small regional companies. He also has to keep track of incoming funds and take legal action when they're not forthcoming.

One of the reasons that the major companies have a lock on distribution is that the task requires incredible expertise—nothing less than near encyclopedic knowledge of virtually all of the theaters in the world. For Meyer, the job is scaled down slightly, since many theaters won't take a Russ Meyer film under any circumstance. Still, he has to know the ones that will.

In the last few years the number of theaters open to Meyer have been dwindling, due to the blockbuster mentality. Many theater owners shy away from low-budget, special-audience movies, preferring the big movie, which appeals to a broader audience. This means that Meyer has to fight for bookings, at least initially.

Instead of opening nationwide on one day, Meyer will usually open in just one city. He will personally supervise the ad campaign, then appear there himself, with an actress or two to generate publicity. If this strategy works and the film does well, theater owners in other cities will be less resistant to his film.

Since the theaters usually pay Meyer a percentage of the box office take, and because theater owners are notoriously slow about these things, earnings take months, even years, to trickle back to Meyer. Once there, however, distributor Meyer can always be counted on to give producer Meyer a fair shake—something that isn't all that common elsewhere.

One last point about distribution: Whereas studios assign thousands of people worldwide to this chore, Meyer gets by on considerably less. When a new film of his is in release, his dozen or so subdistributors handle it in their own regions (as with almost any endeavor, the more restricted the turf, the easier it is to acquire expertise), but when no new film is out and Meyer is just dealing in his previously released films, his "distribution arm" has been known to consist of just one person, working one day a week, taking calls, answering correspondence, billing, and threatening to sue if the bills aren't paid.

The Toll

Whatever else he may be, Meyer is not totally tasteless. His moviegoing is not confined to porno. He sees—and occasionally admires—high-budget films. Sometimes he even envies them, but he's trapped into making "Russ Meyer movies."

Like all independents, Meyer finds it's harder and harder to compete with studio product, largely because most of that product is presold—known by the public because it is a sequel or remake, or based on a best-seller, or featuring a well-known character, or populated with big-name stars. Meyer, too, can indulge in preselling, based on his name, but that's the real pitfall.

A film with Meyer's name on it creates certain expectations among the small segment of the mass audience that knows of him, and he feels compelled to try to fulfill his audience's expectations. On occasions when he hasn't—*The Seven Minutes* and *Blacksnake*, neither of which featured a bustline greater than forty inches—Meyer has seen his audience desert him.

Even when Meyer diverges only slightly from his bawdy format, as he did with the sadomasochistic *Up*, he has trouble filling the theater. The irony is that the man who is his own boss, someone who can go out and make a movie happen all by himself, is virtually enslaved by his audience's taste. And, since Meyer's crude setup has no room for anything as sophisticated as market research, Meyer can only give his public what *he thinks* it wants; then he must wait months or years for their verdict.

Making the stakes even higher is the fact that Meyer does not have access to unlimited funds. Two or, at the most, three losses in a row and his career is over.

3

THE GROUND CREW

THE PEOPLE BEHIND THE SCENES MAY NOT GET THEIR PICTURE IN *People* magazine as often as the stars who show up on the screen, but the ground crew are the people who make the movies fly. Stars may come and go, but those who see to the details of picture making are a continuing, indispensable part of the process.

Naturally there is quite a gap in the number of people involved in making a movie at a major studio—or even an active mini-major—and a small independent producer. And there is even a vast difference between the multifaceted Disney empire and the smaller-scale operation of Paramount. Internally, variations and quirks in the way they work distinguish studios from each other. Despite all these differences, the model we outline here offers a working guide to those who make up the ground crew at a major studio.

Each of the major studios has between 500 and 3,000 full-time employees. The roster covers a broad spectrum: different kinds of jobs, different kinds of people, and vastly different pay rates. Janitors, and even plumbers, are full-time employees. So are lawyers and accountants.

Monetarily, studios are known for paying huge salaries to their highest executives, while keeping the pay scales fairly lean for the lower echelons. They can do this because so many people are clamoring to work at the studios. Eighteen thousand jobs are all that exist in the mainstream of the business, according to one executive in Paramount's personnel department. He goes on to estimate that anywhere from 100,000 to 200,000 people would be qualified to hold those jobs.

All the studios are dependent on television production, many for more than half of their business. The two media divide the studios into dual hierarchies: TV executives and film executives, with the film executives usually enjoying greater status.*

Serving both hierarchies is a large, mostly unionized support staff, consisting of secretaries, other kinds of office workers, lawyers, negotiators, maintenance and security people, and many more. Also on the lot are a number of seminomadic producers, there for one film, off to somewhere else for the next, sometimes surrounding themselves with scores of their own employees who are loyal to the producer, rather than to the studio.

For some on the lot, working for a studio is just another job; for others, thanks to union seniority, it can be a soft featherbed. But for many more, the workaholic ethic prevails: ten hours at the office, more hours attending studio screenings, then still more time at home, reading scripts or making telephone calls.

The Filmmaking Process

Perhaps the best way to highlight the various permanent employees in the studio system is to follow the course of a hypothetical film as it goes from idea to money-earning entity. Since there has never been any one film that has been typical in every way, the example that has been

---

*However, several major studios are now headed by former executives of the television division.

constructed will incorporate the broadest ranges of experiences that a film can go through on its way to the screen.

THE AGENT

The inclusion of the agent in a chapter about studio personnel may seem out of place, for agents are independent operators who owe allegiance to no particular studio; yet they are a part of the system. One of the reasons for their debatable status comes from the intense emotions that ride on the task of finding work. If the agent gets his client a job, he seems to be an agent in the truest sense of the word: someone who is working for someone else. In reality, though, the agent, especially the script seller, is a middleman. Unlike a lawyer, he will not necessarily fight for his client to the bitter end. How can he? He's got twenty other clients, any one of whom might be working on deals for the same studio. By law an agent gets 10 percent of his client's earning, but unless he is spectacularly unperceptive, he knows that the real source of the money lies not with his ostensible clients, but with the studios (or the producers). So, with so few sources of money around, there's considerable pressure on agents not to alienate the buyers for the sake of one deal.

The agents serve two valuable functions for the studios. First, they find talent, and second, they screen out some of the really bad stuff. In performing these tasks, they are the studios' first line of defense against the flaky folk from the hinterlands, whose unsolicited manuscripts arrive daily at the studios and are usually returned unread.

THE READERS

Say an agent finds a script he likes. The studios are set up to respond to him via their literary departments. These departments are each made up of a handful of people who spend their days reading and critiquing literary properties.

Although the avowed purpose of the literary department is to discover good writing, most of the time they merely screen out the vast majority of submissions. There's nothing wrong with that, for much of the writing is probably not very good. But even with the materials the literary department recommends, very little happens. It's rare that one film a year per studio will have begun its life as a submission to the literary department. It's hard to say, then, why these departments exist, except perhaps as a way of training future executives or getting certain scripts read and synopsized.

These certain scripts go directly from producers and well-connected agents to the executives, who, in turn, hire readers to synopsize them. These are the scripts that have a real chance of getting made into films, often because by the time the literary department sees them, stars have shown an interest or some of the financing may already have been acquired.

THE HEAD OF THE LITERARY DEPARTMENT

The scripts recommended by the readers are next read by the head of the literary department. Even if he likes a particular script or novel, it still means next to nothing. He must still get the approval of someone above him, often one or more executives, who are sometimes called production vice-presidents. Before going on to them, however, it's important to note that the literary department does have its share of power, chiefly in being able at least to say no to anything and every-thing. The oft-repeated quote is that no one ever got fired for saying no, and the conclusion that can be drawn from such a remark is predictably confusing. In most businesses it would make sense to fire someone who rejected what later turned out to be a profitable idea. If it is that person's job to ferret out good ideas and he passes on one, then perhaps he shouldn't be where he is. By ignoring this logic, the film business is in effect saying that no one can really ever tell whether or not a script will make a hit movie—at least, until the movie is released.

THE VICE-PRESIDENTS

The titles vary, but they all describe an elite position that combines executive savvy with creative flair. Much of the vice-president's time is spent evaluating creative proposals. Some proposals (novels, scripts, and so on) come from the literary department, but others—the ones usually taken more seriously—come directly from producers. (To go into the studio and deal on the vice-presidential level, a producer needs either a track record or some sort of personal relationship with a vice-president.)

Often, the vice-presidents will generate ideas themselves. A newspaper article might suggest a feature film, and the veep will then hire a writer to crank out an outline. Thus begins the writing process, or development, with the veep riding herd on it. Just as often, however, the vice-president will do little more than say yes or no to a project that has already been completely written and fully cast.

If he says no to an idea, script, package, or completed film that has been offered to the studio for distribution, that's the end of that. But if there's a positive response, nothing will happen unless further steps are taken. (There are other veeps, but we'll discuss them later.)

THE HEAD OF PRODUCTION

The head of production, who might also be called a vice-president, coordinates the input from his veeps. After he has read the hypothetical script and approved it, it will be passed on to the president. The head of production also oversees all the films that are being shot by the studio.

THE PRESIDENT

The president is the one who says yes or no. Often, before deciding, he'll ask to see a budget so he'll know if the film is worth making *at that price.* He also controls the purse strings and has vast administrative responsibilities. (More on him later.)

BUSINESS AFFAIRS

At this point the script might be optioned, a deal where the studio offers a few thousand dollars to the writer in return for the exclusive right to consider purchasing the script during a given period of time. While the majority of options never blossom into actual screenplay sales, each option contract must contain provisions for all sorts of unlikely contingencies. Putting these down on paper are the people at business affairs, who negotiate with agents.

Although the broad strokes of the deal have been sketched by the vice-presidents, or perhaps the president, the business affairs people are the ones who must fill in the specifics. In most negotiations precedence is extremely important. How much did this writer get for his last script, how much do first-time writers get, how much was offered by another studio? The business affairs people don't have an entirely free hand to negotiate, since they have ceilings, both in terms of money and in common sense. Though it is rare for a deal to be blown by an obstinate representative of the business affairs department, it does happen on occasion. Also, somewhat surprisingly, since it's not cash out of their own pockets, the business affairs people don't just lay out their ceiling figure to the agents and say take it or leave it. Instead, like negotiators everywhere else, they'll bargain for the best possible deal for those they represent.

THE LEGAL DEPARTMENT

Once a contract has been agreed upon, it will be set into legal form by lawyers employed by the studio. These lawyers also handle all the other legal matters that involve the studio, but contract writing seems to be their most frequent duty. These contracts are then read by the lawyers of our hypothetical writer.

PAYROLL

Assuming the contract is agreeable to everyone, the next step is for the writer to receive his check from the payroll department. (Actually, the agent receives the check, takes out his 10 percent, and then sends the rest to his client.) Payroll, naturally, pays everyone else at the studio, too.

THE BUDGET DEPARTMENT

Next, a tentative budget for the film might be drawn up by the budget department. Depending on the studio, the budget can be done within that department or it might be sent out to the various back lot departments for individualized estimates, if the studio does not have a budget department.

THE BACK LOT DEPARTMENTS

These are the last vestiges of the booming movie factory days, when most of the physical work of moviemaking went on within the confines of the studio lots. Today, each department may consist of just one full-time, salaried employee. But, as a source in the personnel office put it, "If we have to shoot a scene with a big water tank in it, you can bet there'll be fifty plumbers working here that day."

Besides the plumbing department, there are departments for camera, wardrobe, props, construction, special effects, paint, electrical operations, machinery, engineering, labor, transportation, safety engineering, crafts services (such as woodworking), postproduction, and operations (which coordinates these back lot departments).

Someone in each department reads the script from the point of view of what will be needed from his department. He then turns an estimate in to the budget department or the operations desk, and a final figure is soon tallied. That number then goes right back to the president, who may then decide to give the project his go-ahead.

If the studio is one of those that are small pieces of big conglomerates, the leadership of the conglomerate may want to have a say about how its millions are going to be invested. This does not always happen, but one source suggested that the conglomerates leave the studios alone as long as the studios make money. A second source, a vice-president, pointed out that the studio leadership knows how its conglomerate owners think and learns to think that way itself. Ergo, no hassles.

So, the president gives the go-ahead to the script, and over the next year or two, it is hoped that their hailstone will turn into a huge snowball.

"THE VEEPS" (AGAIN)

Since this particular script was brought to the attention of the studio by a vice-president in production, this veep will oversee the project from beginning to end. At the point that the purchase of the script has been approved, the veep must hire a producer. This is not the most common flow of action, but we use it to illustrate the parameters of the veep's power. He can, in effect, perform duties very similar to a producer himself, in that he can be the one who combines the major creative elements of a film. Once a producer is brought in, however, much of the power is usurped by that producer, and the veep remains as the overseer on behalf of the studio. He will be the one who comments on the writing as it develops from a scanty outline to a detailed shooting script.

THE PRESIDENT (AGAIN)

Finally, the script is acceptable to all in the studio hierarchy, as well to as the outsiders (producer, director, and stars). It is up to the president, at this time, to secure financing for the film. Often, this money comes from profits made by the studio's other films. In such a case, it's basically a matter of turning on the tap. In other instances, the money can come from a variety of sources: outside investors, banks, or even other studios, as a way to spread the risk. Negotiations for this sort of financing are carried on by the president.

Once into production, the head of production oversees and coordinates all the studio's production. The president oversees *him*, and the chairman of the board oversees the president.

PREPRODUCTION

Typically during this phase the production team will use office space at the studio but not too many studio personnel. Studios have casting departments, but these departments usually specialize in TV work. As with most of the creative aspects of moviemaking, the work of finding actors to appear in films is done by independent companies. These companies are hired by the producers and given the script of the movie they are hired to cast. Those doing the casting then contact agents and, finally, their choices are submitted to the producer and director for approval. Finding marquee names to fill in the major roles is not usually a job for the casting director; instead, the producer, and occasionally the director, must rely on his own bargaining skills to attract these assets to his film.

PRODUCTION

During a period of active feature and TV production, the employee role of a studio can swell to 5,000. Many of these workers will be crewmen (cameramen, soundmen, makeup, and so forth), brought in on a day-by-day basis to work on the production. The back lot departments expand on a similar temporary basis to accommodate the work at hand. The hiring of all this additional personnel, as well as the more permanent employees, is handled by the personnel department. The job is a mixed blessing for those who work in this department. Because so many people want jobs in the business—any jobs—it is not hard to fill vacancies. In fact, according to a source in 20th Century-Fox's personnel department, some individuals are so eager to get into the studios that they offer to work for free. They are not hired.

All this eager availability carries a special irony for the personnel people, because it means that they aren't paid as highly as they would be if they were doing accounting or personnel work for, say, IBM or Exxon.

PUBLICITY

The studios all have publicity departments, which are designed to get free media attention for films. Publicists invite print and TV journalists onto movie sets, get magazines and newspapers to interview their stars, and occasionally dream up weird publicity stunts. They also field requests for interviews from journalists. Like the casting department, however, studio publicity often finds itself usurped by outside companies hired by the producers. The duties of the publicity department, on a particular film, begin prior to production and end only when the film is well into its run at the theaters.

POSTPRODUCTION

The studios employ scores of people in the field of postproduction. While the editors are hired to work on one film at a time, special effects technicians, sound mixers, recordists, and projectionists can find steady work at the studios. Their security there usually depends on union seniority. Much of their labor is for TV series.

THE LABS

Some labs, such as the M-G-M lab, are owned outright by the studios and located on the same lot, while others are parts of the same conglomerates, or totally independent. Their main duty is to develop the negatives that come from the camera, make positive prints from them, and then, when the film has been edited, make prints—often in the hundreds—to be shipped to the theaters. Lab workers are unionized, and there is a distinct hierarchy. First there are the administrative and supervisory personnel. Then there are the timers, men who control the color balance in the prints. It's a job akin to adjusting a color TV set, but much of its difficulty stems from the numerous variables and the possibility of wasting print after expensive print. The prestige of this job rests on the fact that the timer constantly makes artistic decisions (albeit small ones), such as deciding to give a sequence a brown, earthy tone, or perhaps making a scene seem dark and moody. Printers, next in the hierarchy, operate a machine that's a bit like a very complicated movie projector but that does not throw a picture anywhere. Instead, a tiny light shines through a moving negative and exposes moving print stock. These machines are usually run in almost total darkness.

Near the bottom of this ladder are those who operate film developing machines, huge complicated affairs, with multigallon tanks of chemicals and film running intestinelike through them. Finally, there are the personnel who put the film onto projection reels and then into the metal cans that protect it on its way to the theaters.

DISTRIBUTION

The distribution area of a studio is usually a worldwide network of hundreds of workers, organized in regional units. Their main duty is to get the movies to the theaters, as well as coordinate all the advertising efforts for a film. Each regional distribution office may have as few as one or two employees. Back home at the studio, the head of distribution, often a president or vice-president, will work out selling and advertising strategies, sometimes in concert with marketing researchers or, more frequently, by instinct based on years of experience.

The field offices of the studio have one other important function: They try to keep the theater owners honest. They make in-person trips to the theaters to see for themselves how their films are doing, and they collect what is due them from the box office receipts.

THE FINANCIAL DEPARTMENT

When the proceeds from a film start to come in, they go first to the financial department, a bottomless pit, according to some filmmakers who've had shares of profits that never quite seemed to materialize. The accountants who work in this department are responsible for keeping track of the studio's income and expenditures, as well as indirectly informing lots of directors, actors, and writers that this is not the year for the new Ferrari.

ADMINISTRATION

Close to half the permanent workers at any studio are secretaries. These are women (mostly) who are not necessarily relatives, lovers, or friends of anyone but who have come into their jobs through such easily tested secretarial skills as typing and taking dictation. Many of them become trusted right hands to their bosses, but it is unusual for them to jump from the administrative branch to any other.

Other administration departments include security (the guards), corporate insurance, merchandising and licensing (getting movie themes into other products, such as toys, T-shirts, and games), and music (some of the studios have their own record labels). These departments, along with the upkeep of the lot itself, are all paid for out of the profits of the studio's filmmaking.

The budget of each studio film has an item called overhead, which is designed to pay for all these activities. With most studios, it's an extra percentage tacked on to the final budget, an amount as small as 5 percent or as great as 30 percent. When the proceeds come in from the theaters, the studios are reimbursed for the money they actually spent producing the film, and they get this extra amount.

Working at the Studios

As noted before, studio jobs run the gamut. They often require long, grueling hours, but sometimes an employee will find nothing but time on his hands. Lower- and middle-level salaries are usually a bit skimpy, but unionized employees are well paid and receive considerable fringe benefits. For them, however, seasonal employment and occasional layoffs can make their salaries seem smaller.

Studio employees have to deal with a hierarchy that tends to freeze them into their departments. For example, a personnel man we talked to wanted to go into production, but he felt that only by going to a different studio did he have a chance of making the transition. He's still waiting to make his move. Also still waiting is a male secretary who found that his job at Universal got him into close contact with a number of producers and directors, who he hoped would help him up the ladder. He, too, wanted to get into production. In fact, almost everybody does. Though employees tend to complain about being trapped in their various departments, most are really upset at not being allowed into the production branch. Perhaps the situation was consciously designed to make sure the ground crew don't all become pilots.

A second criticism, more serious, is voiced by some studio personnel. A lawyer in one of the studios' legal departments summed it up by saying the film business had a garment industry mentality, that "if a guy was good enough for them to hire, he's good enough for us."

This lateral mobility (and lack of vertical mobility) is seen most commonly in the production division, with executives moving from studio to studio with such frequency that many don't get to see the release of films they initiated. Moreover, many of the executives take whole teams with them. A president might bring his veeps, his head of production, and so forth. So, then, security is not one of the attractions of working for a studio.

Beyond that, though, is a far more troubling point: Just as artistic, well-reviewed films are not always rewarded by the public going to see them, good workers aren't always helped up the ladder at the studios. There are workers who are promoted out of the mailrooms and they rise meteorically, but they are rare. Such workers are a threat to the people at the top of the hierarchy. Since much of these executives' work is based on opinion and taste, and since almost everyone has lots of opinions (if not taste), there are a lot of people who think there's room for them at the top. A frozen hierarchy puts a stop to that sort of thinking.

Status

There's an intangible that often throws the movie factory model in chaos. That intangible is status. Status is usually based on association with successful films but can also flow from having a well-received novel, being someone's consort, having a relative in the business, or any one of a number of other circumstances. Once status is filtered into the system, the model works differently—less so at the lower levels, more so at the higher ones.

A director with a hit film does not come as a supplicant to a studio. He will more likely make a deal directly with the president of the studio. From then on, it's the director's film, and he controls it all the way through shooting, editing, and even advertising.

An agent representing a hot novelist considers himself a failure if the novel is read by a mere reader in the story department. If he has any real influence, the novel will be read by the president himself.

Most writing work is not in the form of unsolicited screenplays; writers are, instead, hired by the studios (and producers). They are hired usually because of their track record. One screenwriter told us that there are only about 300 writers who have written more than one film. The group of "produced writers" is tiny, then—but this small band is well paid and usually working.

More often than not, the producer supplies the creative impetus. Typically the producer will read, say, a novel, submitted by an agent (or bought from a bookstore), and then option it, or instead, go to the studio and ask it to option it for him. Or he may hire a writer to write a screenplay based on the producer's idea, then get stars interested, and possibly even arrange some of the financing. Agents also purchase scripts and sell them to studios.

In theory, it is possible that the only studio personnel to come in contact with a so-called studio production would be the top executives and the distribution department.

Finally, to bring up one last quirk of the system, the film may have been given the go-ahead by one team of executives but released after a changing of the guard. The result might be that the new team would feel estranged from the project begun by their predecessors, and they might give this film a smaller ad and publicity campaign than one of their own, or they might even cancel the project altogether.

The Foot in the Door

Although, as we've seen, the studio system offers a wide range of work, production is the area that seems to attract the most outsiders. As a result, it is exceedingly difficult to get a job in production.

Other types of jobs are more or less open to the public through the personnel office, especially those requiring specific skills picked up in other industries: secretarial, accounting, and legal. It's not impossible for persistent outsiders to come off the street and get these jobs, but once again, it helps to know someone. One way to avoid getting stuck at the bottom of the ladder is to find, say, secretarial work with one of those production companies that are on the lot just to make one film. It's not absolutely essential to know someone in order to get one of these jobs, but most of the time the only way openings are publicized is through a personal grapevine.

Within these smaller organizations, there seems to be a little more fluidity in the hierarchy and more chance for personal contact with the boss. The problem with this approach is a lack of security: Small production companies are not known for their longevity.

A law degree or a personal fortune are both tangible things, the best possible reference. With lengthy contracts designed to deal with every possible contingency becoming more and more common, an increasing number of lawyers are arriving at studios, often from entertainment law firms but occasionally directly from law school. Since they are intimately involved in deal making, they have a good chance of eventually moving into production.

Money from the outside is a sought-after commodity, but without expertise—perhaps in a partnership of some sort—it won't do much good. One way around that, of course, is to finance one's own movies—if one has enough money.

THE REAL FOOT IN THE DOOR

With overwhelming frequency, the key to that door into which so many want to insert their feet comes from friends, lovers, or relatives. This kind of hiring is consistent with the uncertainty of the business.

Charges of nepotism and cronyism have often been leveled at film business hiring procedures, and for the most part they are true. Hiring one's friends and relatives is a common practice in many businesses, but the prevalence of it in film points to an especially significant characteristic of the industry: insecurity. Nepotism and cronyism are not just ways of doing favors for friends and relatives; they are also ways of surrounding oneself with presumable allies (although allies, and even relatives, have been known to have fallings out). Another reason for this sort of hiring is that in many areas there is no reliable way to screen a potential employee's skills. So why not hire friends and relatives?

Finally, there's the mixture of work and sex. Although actresses do occasionally sleep with agents, producers, or directors for the purpose of landing a role, the blend is usually more subtle than that, especially as it applies to nonacting jobs. Among all the instance of sex becoming intertwined with careers, probably the rarest would be the instances when a career favor is traded for a sexual favor. More often, it comes down to a matter of hiring girlfriends and boyfriends.

This sort of employment practice helps satisfy the executive's need for loyal assistants and has an added benefit, too: It keeps the lover financially beholden.

As for those who get a job because of whose bed they share, there tends to be surprisingly little cynicism. Though it may appear to be mutual exploitation to outsiders, such relationships are usually perceived by those in them as personal and professional partnerships, the one indistinguishable from the other, just as in many movie deals which *don't* involve sex.

As Michael Corleone of *The Godfather* put it, "It's *all* personal."

4

DID SOMEBODY
SAY HOLLYWOOD?

TOURISTS WHO ARE DRAWN TO HOLLYWOOD ARE INEVITABLY DISAP-
pointed. The uninformed show up at Hollywood and Vine and see
nothing but tacky tourist traps and hookers of both sexes breathing in
a lot of brown smog. Visitors find it hard to imagine that at that very
corner, and nearby as well, movies are happening.

To understand the position of the area called Hollywood to the film
business, a bit of Los Angeles geography is in order. Like all major
cities, Los Angeles has a downtown area that is home to the city
government, the courts, two daily newspapers, and some major corporate headquarters. Sections of downtown look like New York City—
so much so that they have doubled for the Big Apple on some TV
shows. Aside from shooting there, though, film industry types steer
clear of downtown.

Downtown L.A. *was* Los Angeles in the 1880s, but the city's expansion changed all that. Downtown is now a daytime district, packed
with people during the workday but a ghost town at night. Meanwhile,
the rest of the city has expanded to become an urban sprawl where,
as everybody knows, it's next to impossible to get around on foot.

That's because the city is split into scores of districts, each a complete entity with its own center and outskirts, spread over a vast area that the automobile helped to conquer . . . and divide. Hollywood is one such entity.

Yet despite its reputation as an ultramodern "car city," L.A. gets much of its character from its topography. Hills, valleys, canyons, and the beach all help shape people's attitudes toward the city, and in the movie business, even nature carries status.

Arguably, the most prestigious address in the film community is Malibu, in the northwestern part of L.A. County. Needless to say, Malibu's beachfront homes are expensive, but then again, it wouldn't be prestigious unless it were expensive and exclusive. A small section of Malibu, the Colony, is located along a thin strip of sand that completely vanishes during storms. Houses, then, are inundated by the tide unless the owners have had the foresight to stack sandbags on their patios.

Most of the year, though, Malibu is a dream. The Colony is loaded with younger entertainment heavyweights, and the rest of the beach, though technically public, has no easy access to visitors and virtually no parking spaces. The place has a resortlike atmosphere, quiet and relaxed on the surface and just the same underneath. Rock stars live here, along with actors and some especially successful writers and executives. The beach air is usually smogless, often the only part of L.A. that is.

Malibu has something in common with most of the other status addresses: It's hard to get to. It seems that in Los Angeles, accessibility has an inverse ratio to the quality of the neighborhood. Witness the location of the other status neighborhoods: the narrow, winding "beach" canyons, such as Topanga, that cut through the mountains separating the western San Fernando Valley from the beaches. Here, country-style living is offered to industry types who have a slightly counterculture air to their image. Ranches with horses and chickens are available, but so are humbler accommodations for those who haven't made it yet. Interestingly, given their entertainment slant, these semirural communities, and Malibu as well, are a long forty-five minutes from Hollywood even when traffic is flowing smoothly.

Nearer Hollywood are the other canyons, Laurel, Coldwater, and Bendict, which all cut over the hills separating the Valley from Beverly Hills (on the west) and West Hollywood (on the east). Intersecting these canyons at the crest of the hills is Mulholland Drive, still another posh address. Like the other neighborhoods, these areas have narrow, winding roads and are also at the mercy of nature. When it rains, houses are either beseiged by sliding mud or hammered by torrents of water. During the dry, late summer months, forest fires race through the canyons as well as the mountain areas near the beach. The lush vegetation that makes these areas seem so desirable in spring becomes dry tinder in summer.

The so-called valley canyons, though by no means inexpensive, can be afforded by occupants of middle-level-prestige echelons: actors whose faces are familiar but whose names you don't know, TV writers and directors, and a few of the younger executive types.

The hills then merge into Beverly Hills, and also Holmby Hills, expensive residential areas, where the older and most established talent and executives often live.

Below, in the nonhilly part of Beverly Hills—called the "flats" by locals—are quiet, broad streets lined with trees and old, elegant two-story houses. This neighborhood, though expensive, defies the rule of accessibility. It is very accessible by car, but any security threat posed by that situation is ably handled by the Beverly Hills Police Department, long known for their eagerness to stop anyone who looks "out of place."

Pacific Palisades, Brentwood, and Bel Air are all prestige addresses, too, but less trendy than Malibu, the canyons, or Beverly Hills.

Westwood Village is an especially interesting story. Unlike most of Los Angeles, it is a pedestrian district densely packed with shops, restaurants, and movie theaters. It is, in fact, L.A.'s only first-run movie theater area, excepting a handful of first-run theaters on Hollywood Boulevard and in isolated Century City.

On weekend nights, the sidewalks in the Village are jammed, a smaller-scale version of the crowds that pass on foot through New

York, London, and Paris. The Village is adjacent to the campus of the University of California, at Los Angeles, and because of the large student population, a Westwood Village address has very little prestige. Most of the homes are apartments, anyway. Westwood proper, the area that surrounds the Village, has a lot of larger, older two-story homes, in a basically conservative neighborhood favored by attorneys and young doctors on the way up. The Village has a bustling, urban charm, but few show-biz types stay in the nearby hotels. More likely, they'll pick the Beverly Hills Hotel or the Beverly Wilshire, situated on Wilshire Boulevard, one of the most expensive shopping areas in the city.

Up and coming as an address for movie industry denizens is Venice. Located on the ocean about ten miles south of Malibu, Venice, California, was designed at the turn of the century to mimic Venice, Italy. Today, shallow canals cut through Venice, while old, shabby houses stand shoulder to shoulder with new, quarter-of-a-million-dollar homes. Venice was a low-income combination ghetto and bohemian community in the late 1960s, but by the mid 1970s, one of two things happened: Either L.A.'s more affluent types became intrigued with Venice's color and started moving there, or Venice's hippies suddenly decided that affluence wasn't so bad after all. Most long-term residents of Venice prefer the former explanation, and they're not happy about it. Whatever the reason, the influx of upwardly mobile show-business movers and shakers threatens to drive living costs in Venice out of the reach of the people who moved there in the 1960s.

North Hollywood is a dreary, light industrial and tract community, farther from Hollywood than its name suggests, on the other side of the Hollywood Hills. This is the kind of place where established low- and middle-level film people live. Long-term studio secretaries have apartments here, along with crew people and an occasional young employee of the studio story department. Increasingly, many movie supply companies are springing up in North Hollywood, drawn by the area's close proximity to Universal, Disney, and the Burbank Studios.

West Hollywood is, indeed, west of Hollywood. It, too, is primarily for hopefuls rather than the established, but it is far different in atmosphere from North Hollywood. West Hollywood is a neighborhood of small, Spanish-style houses; apartments; antique stores; tiny, chic restaurants and boutiques; a block or so of heavily concentrated porn theaters and shops, and a very visible gay element. Any male who lives in this neighborhood runs a certain risk of having his address double as a hint of his sexual proclivities.

Hollywood itself is a large and varied neighborhood, located west of downtown. In the eastern part of Hollywood, along Western Avenue, there is a large porno district and also a large, mixed minority community. In the hills, the Hollywood Hills, there are old houses and apartments to rent, ideal for actors and actresses who have just started to make it. Higher in the hills there is an exclusive, hidden-away residential district, as well the famous HOLLYWOOD sign. On the flatlands are still more old apartments and houses in the Spanish style, but this is a low-prestige neighborhood.

Living in Hollywood itself are a lot of film-lab employees, unestablished crew hopefuls, and a throng of aspiring actors and actresses. That's not to say that Hollywood's only residents are aspiring actors— rather, that the locale is a chosen place to live for many of them.

It's been occasionally said that movies are not made in Hollywood anymore, that they are instead produced in Burbank (Warner Brothers, Columbia, and Disney), Universal City (Universal Studios), Culver City (M-G-M), and Rancho Park (20th Century-Fox). This is rubbish.

More than any other single district of L.A., Hollywood is still the leader in movies. True, most of the major studio lots are clustered around Hollywood, rather than in Hollywood itself, but that doesn't mean that Hollywood has fallen out of the film business.

Three movie lots are located within the Hollywood city limits. First is the Samuel Goldwyn Studio—which is not a producer or a distributor, but does play host to an occasional feature and TV series. It was recently purchased by Warner Brothers. Then there is Paramount— a major producer and distributor, with a busy schedule of TV and features. Finally, there are the Hollywood General Studios, sound stages and offices currently owned by Francis Coppola's Omni-Zoe-trope Company.

But it takes more than studios to make movies. Hollywood is filled with small companies that provide production and postproduction services and supplies. Remember Republic Studios, the company that made all of those westerns and serials in the 1940s? That institution has evolved into Consolidated Film Industries (CFI), a large film lab that develops film, makes prints, and does some optical work for features. Its sprawling plant is right in the heart of Hollywood. Other labs occupy storefronts along such thoroughfares as Sunset Boulevard and Santa Monica Boulevard. Many of them serve feature filmmakers, but others will take on work for student filmmakers and amateurs.

Eastman Kodak, the world's leading supplier of unexposed film, has a warehouse and an office in Hollywood. Camera and equipment rental shops abound. Editing rooms are tiny enough to fit in virtually everywhere; they're scattered all over Hollywood. Screening rooms and postproduction sound services seem to be everywhere, too. Western Costume, the largest collection of rentable costumes in the world, is located in Hollywood too, as are the offices of some independent distributors, agents, and producers—though the latter two groups seem to gravitate more toward Beverly Hills.

Finally, Hollywood Boulevard is home to the so-called "Boulevard audience," a supposed mix of blacks and Chicanos who come in from the ghettos and barrios of central and east Los Angeles to see action movies. As such, they are considered a barometer of national urban minority taste. Aside from sizing these people up as a potential audience, industry regulars all but ignore them. Cynics claim it's a sort of trade-off whereby the children of Chicanos and blacks stay out of the film business and the children of movie executives don't join street gangs. Despite occasional efforts to recruit minorities, white males still retain most of the decision-making power in the industry. This may begin to change when (and if) the federal government starts to enforce civil rights legislation in the film industry. All government suppliers fall under the purview of these laws, and the studios are government suppliers by virtue of their distribution of films to military bases.

Hollywood—figurative Hollywood—for all the business it does and all its supposed influence, has much less pull with the government—federal, state, and local—than any of dozens of other industries.

Whereas other industries doggedly lobby for beneficial laws, the movie business is more often than not a passive constituency on which the laws are imposed. Why does this happen? One observer likens the film business to a traveling carnival that sets up its tents, takes its money from the customers, then moves on to the next town. This mentality, a hangover from the early days of the industry, leaves little room for thought of the future, but that's exactly what's needed in order to influence the government at all levels. When other big industries set out to lobby for a piece of legislation, they may plan a campaign that could last as long as twenty years, a campaign conducted every day.

In the film business any activity of that duration would be highly unlikely. The business and the public tastes it rests on are entirely too unstable. Moreover, the internal structures of the individual studios are also too unstable. Since the beginning of the industry there has been a tradition of personalized, concentrated power, and that means that dealing with a studio is not like dealing with other kinds of companies, which have, for the most part, institutionalized decision making by committee. Dealing with a studio means dealing with individuals, with all their attendant quirks. These individuals don't tend to be around all that long, either, and that's another problem: In order to forge alliances, long-term political stability and a sense of permanence are absolutely essential. Finally, the spirit of competition goes a long way toward preventing unified action on the part of the studios.

So much for the potential federal clout of the film industry. But surely things should be different on the municipal level. Surely there is a realization not only of film's cultural value, but of its importance as an industry? Wrong. Neither Hollywood proper nor Los Angeles is anywhere close to being the film industry's company town.

Hollywood itself is not a self-governing entity. It is part of the city of Los Angeles, which is run by a city council and a mayor whose powers are generally said to be slightly more limited than those of the mayors of other big cities. The mayor does, however, have a large ceremonial role, and Tom Bradley, L.A.'s mayor, has used that role to give considerable public recognition to people in the film industry.

The most common transaction between the industry and city government is a rather trivial one: obtaining permits to shoot on locations throughout the city. The city office that grants these permits is a part of a larger office set up to encourage industrial development in general. The way they are supposed to do this is through facilitating the process of getting permits. This function of the office can apply to the film business in the area of support companies, such as film labs, which require compliance with a myriad of building and safety codes. The office is supposed to cut through some of the red tape inherent in all those laws.

Easy access to location shooting hasn't always been a fact of life in L.A. Initially, of course, film companies shot wherever they could and hoped no one would complain about them (this is still done today, but mainly by the producers of very low-budget films and porno). Later, zoning laws were changed so that films could only be shot in so-called M-2, or light manufacturing, zones. To show the dominance of the studio system at that time, the only M-2 zones were studios. Before the late 1960s, shooting in L.A.'s city streets involved acquiring permission from the local police precincts, an occasionally complicated process.

In the late 1960s, the city of Los Angeles, doing its small part to limit runaway production, liberalized its zoning, so that movies can now be shot anywhere, although permit and use fees are levied. These seldom exceed a few hundred dollars but can rocket to considerably more when the film company has to pay the salaries of city policemen brought out to direct traffic around the film location. These fees must be paid whether the film is shot on city property or on private property.

One discouragement filmmakers face in trying to shoot on public property is the city demands that they protect themselves with enormous insurance policies. Otherwise the rules are fairly liberal. According to one source at the permit office, permits are attainable even for pornographers—"Otherwise, you'd have censorship," said the source.

The same source pointed out that the permit office is self-support-ing, a curious boast, since all it means is that the money goes around in a circle: The employees sell permits so they can get paid to sell more permits. They perform two other duties, though: They coordinate shooting on a first-come, first-served basis, so that two companies do not shoot on the same day at the same location, and they balance the public's right to peace and quiet against the production companies' right to shoot their movies almost anywhere they want.

It is in the latter area that there is the most controversy, and even that isn't much. Mayor Bradley set up an advisory board called the Los Angeles Film Development Commission as a way of linking the city government with the film industry. An unpaid cross section of the industry, the members of this group meet privately once a month. Their main concern seems to be to weigh the complaints of members of the public irritated by companies shooting on location. A Burt Reynolds film may be a curiosity and a major attraction in a small town, but in L.A. the public is jaded to the point where, Burt or no Burt, they want access to their driveways, with no noisy film crew down the street to keep them awake at night. When matters like these come up, the commission acts as sort of a long-term arbitrator, while more immediate problems are handled by a member of the Public Works Commission who is empowered to make on-the-spot arbitration of problems.

The commission, and also the California Motion Picture Office as well as the film boards of other cities and states, serves one other major purpose: promotion. Their goal is to bring filmmakers to their particu-lar areas. The idea behind this, of course, is to attract large quantities of cash to these areas. A film company on location rents lodgings, buys food, hires extras, and generally serves to stimulate the local economy.

Some locales have initiated aggressive campaigns to attract filmmak-ers. Representatives from around the country have been known to come to the major studios hawking the scenery and services of their towns and states. Los Angeles and the state of California have done little of this. Their efforts consist mainly of ad campaigns in trade papers. The benefits they tout are the same benefits that drew the movie pioneers to southern California: fair climate and vastly varying scenery. They also cite one thing that wasn't here before the twentieth century: the film industry itself, with its thousands of support personnel, many eager to help newcomers make their movies.

With so much logistical help, and such a large pool of acting talent available, producers would be foolish to go elsewhere, yet they do, mainly for three reasons: First, they sometimes yearn for totally unfamiliar terrain in order to give the audiences something they haven't seen before. Second, some states have right-to-work laws, which means that producers who are so inclined can hire cheap labor. Finally, some cities and states make it even easier to shoot in those places than it is to shoot in L.A. New York City, for example, doesn't charge producers for the wages of city employees, such as policemen, who are brought in to facilitate filming. As noted before, Los Angeles does.

Los Angeles is not exactly the company town, even though the combined total of film and TV employees, about 60,000, is concentrated there. Other industries employ more (aerospace, 330,000; public education, 400,000), but they are scattered all over four of southern California's most populous counties. Why, then, does the film industry seem to have so little influence with the local government?

One reason often cited is public resistance. When the subject of reducing or eliminating permit and use fees comes up, it is usually dismissed with the suggestion that no politician could support such legislation and still retain favor with his constituency. The public attitude, it is assumed, is something along the lines of "Why give them special treatment?"—the resentment perhaps stirred by the imagined spectacle of rich people getting even richer thanks to favorable legislation. But the assistant cameraman who lives in a tract home down the block, the script girl in the next apartment, and the actor waiting tables are all far removed from the stereotype of the fat producer in his Mercedes. Yet when most people think of the economic side of show business, images of wealth and glamour come to mind first, especially in Los Angeles, where much of that wealth is paraded. Then, too, there's a picture of Sodom-and-Gomorrah-by-the-sea that many people have, a picture most recently reinforced by Roman Polanski and David

Begelman. Who wants to help subsidize *those* people? the voters ask.

As this is written, the industry has just won a concession from the city, one that city officials seemed to think was a major accomplishment: a second city of Los Angeles film permit office was opened. It seems that the studios were tired of sending personnel all the way to the Civic Center downtown. They wanted a more convenient office . . . and what better place for such an office than right in the heart of Hollywood?

5

BUDGETING:

THE HIGH COST
OF REINVENTING
THE WHEEL

RIGHT FROM THE START, THE WAY BUDGETING IS HANDLED IN THE MOVIE business throws a lot of people for a loop. In most other businesses, the money spent manufacturing a product tends to be a meticulously guarded trade secret. Details of compensation agreements, service contracts, and the like are also held close to the corporate vest. Chatting about money in public is looked on by many corporations as either distasteful, dangerous, or both.

It doesn't work that way in Hollywood. Trade publications and the entertainment pages of most large newspapers routinely print handouts announcing the latest budget figures of current films. During the Christmas season of 1979 the collection of science fiction films competing for the holiday box office dollar even used the size of their continually escalating budgets as a promotional technique, reasoning that the larger the budget, the better the special effects potential might seem to the ticket buyer.

It's not just that the budget figures are so blaringly bandied about, either. Most people who are interested in Hollywood are puzzled by the variation in budgets. A film can cost $4 million. Or $45 million.

Independent producers get by with spending anywhere from $250,000 to $970,000. Motion Picture Association of America president Jack Valenti, speaking for the studios, recently announced that the cost of an average studio film now demands an outlay of about $6 million. Most studio sources tell us the figure is roughly $2 million above that amount. Downright odd, actually, to have a product that jumps around in cost so. After all, film in a can is more or less film in a can, right?

Well, no. The fundamental fact about the craft of budgeting is that it deals, in each and every case, with the process of reinventing the wheel. In other words, each film is a prototype and cannot borrow footage or other components from other films. (Unless, of course, there is the rare case of a film and its sequel being produced at the same time, as happened with *The Three Musketeers* among others. In that case, though, the production is budgeted as a single film would be. Where a sequel is produced some time after the original production that spawned it, budgeting must start all over again. Locations will be different, the story has to advance using new events, and so forth. Even where much of the same cast is used, from a budgeting perspective, each of the principals will charge a good deal more for their second appearance.) One of the implications of the movies' prototypical nature is that the fiscal planning logic used in other sorts of endeavors just doesn't apply to films. No film is ever a single unit of assembly-line manufacture. Each film is an individual entity that brings with it a unique set of considerations for those charged with figuring out just how much it's going to cost.*

We're making this point at some length because getting it straight is an essential step in understanding how the actual process of arriving at a budget is accomplished. And that process begins, in the movie business, with the use of a projected budget as a tool to decide whether or not a picture can be produced for the money that is available, or whether it should be abandoned because its cost is too high, relative to its potential audience. The budget departments at the major studios pencil out costs for many movies that are never produced; scores of

*We are indebted to Mr. Hilton Green, executive feature production manager, Universal Studios, for this analysis of the problems he faces.

independents—unless they are stunningly foolhardy—have toned down or given up on their movies because the film they had in mind was of greater dimensions than the money they had in hand.

The script is the catalyst that gets the chore of budgeting going. At the major studios and most of the mini-majors, the studio personnel who are on the hook for ultimate responsibility—vice-president in charge of production, or the chief of the studio—send a script to the budget department, a group of people whose experience equips them to make a good guess at what a movie will cost. Along with the script, the budget department also receives from the studio brass what one budgeteer calls "the ground rules." These tend to be a list of directors, or the type of director the studio has in mind for the picture (how expensive, in other words), and the sort of cast the studio has tentatively selected. The amount of time available to produce the film, to conform to the schedule of the principal cast members, director, or seasonal considerations—it's hard to shoot a ski movie in California in August—is also part of the ground rules.

The first two of these three ground rules cover an area of the budget known as "above the line." Generally, above-the-line costs constitute expenses for what are regarded as the creative aspects of a film, before actual production begins. Buying a script or the rights to a book, hiring stars to act in the film, paying the director's salary or any fees asked by the producer are among the above-the-line costs.

When the approximate amount of money the studio plans to lay out for above-the-line costs is communicated to the budget department, their chief task is to determine what the "below-the-line costs" of the movie will be. These include the costs incurred in the physical production of the movie; the cost of unexposed film stock, building sets, and salaries for the crew are some of the items in the computation of below-the-line debits.

At the major studios, below-the-line costs are gathered during a period of about ten days. During that time, each of the departments on the studio lot—plumbing, electrical, construction, and any other services called for by the script—submit cost estimates to the budget department. Ideally, the director has been chosen at this juncture, since he will be able to give the budget department a clear idea of his requirements. Since most major productions also rely heavily on location shooting, possible locations will be scouted to set an estimate of location fees as well as costs of shooting on location.

All of these figures make up a "guesstimate" of how much money it will take to make the film. This "guesstimate" is submitted to the studio executives. The budget department is primarily an information source; they provide facts about expenses or offer advice for trimming the budget. The decisions concerning whether or not to allocate production money, and how much, rest with the production bosses. Once the "guesstimate" arrives on the desks of the production bosses, there is usually a tinkering session or two. The studio will try to convince the director that his film can be made for less money; the director will say that he needs one hundred Indians, not forty-five, to create the effect he must have.

"We just sit with the director and the production people and discuss areas where, without hurting the picture, we can bring the budget back into line," comments a diplomatic budgeting veteran at a major studio.

Clearly, if the director comes to the studio with a string of hits, the studio will consider it the better part of valor to authorize a budget that is greater than the production cost they had earlier anticipated. On the other hand, a novice director will usually cooperate in trimming the budget "guesstimate," staying up late at night with the writer in an attempt to tell the same story for less money. However, as paymaster, the studio has lurking in the background the right simply to walk away from a project because they deem a "guesstimate" too high.

"Perhaps a director could use fewer sets or take three days instead of five to shoot one scene—that kind of thing," explains the head of a budget department. "Maybe the studio will say all right to a little more money. We try to advise as to how to come to a meeting of the minds."

(It is an old truth in Hollywood that simply cutting the length of the script won't help much if the budget looks like it will be too high. Just one scene, even one line, can cost a lot of money. There is an equally old Hollywood joke, in which the director tells his tired cast and crew: "We have only one scene to shoot today—the charge of the Light Brigade.")

Once that meeting of the minds has taken place, the budget department types up a budget. There is no such thing as a typical budget, just as there is no such thing as a typical film. Budgets may be only a few pages long or a hundred pages or more of single-spaced columns of figures, with separate budgets for stunts and special effects. The typed budget is then signed by the budget department, the producer, the studio, and, sometimes, the director. While it is not a binding legal document, the signed budget serves as insurance against a director or producer claiming that he thought he had a few million dollars more to work with than the studio had in fact authorized.

The budget is monitored once production begins. The budget department sees all the bills each production runs up on a daily basis. Movies shot on the studio back lot are tracked by reports filed by each of the various departments. Location shooting is watched by the unit manager, who reports expenses and verifies the claims of cast and crew that they did indeed put in a full day of work.

This barrage of daily debits is recorded on a "report card." The report card carries such expenditure data as the cost of the film to date, the estimated cost of the film to date, and any expense categories that are over the budget. Usually, budget overruns are the result of problems that could not be anticipated before actual shooting began. But often it is possible to see these problems coming a day or two in advance—bad weather or hours of overtime for the hairdresser—and the items that are over the budget can be approved in those cases by the studio heads without creating a flap. When a picture runs into large budget overruns, a number of corrective actions can be taken. Should the director be able to make a convincing case for the additional expenses, these may be approved as a matter of course. A more usual procedure is to hammer out a compromise with the director, pointing out that he may not be approaching the production of the movie in the same way in which he said he would. Lastly, of course, the studio can abort the project, figuring that it is better to cut a loss than throw good money after bad. In rare cases these days—although it was fairly common during the heyday of the studio system—a studio will replace a director who they feel is not competent to complete the picture within the budget. These options are mulled over after an estimate of the amount of money it will take to complete the film is submitted by the budget department.

Assuming that the production continues more or less on course, the budget department is responsible for another critical fiscal document. About ninety days after the movie has been completed—shot, edited, scored—the budget department submits what is called a final. This is what the film actually cost to make, a figure also known as *negative cost*, the amount of money spent to get a negative of the finished film. When it is said in public or in print that the budget for a given film is $35 million, it is usually the final that is being referred to.

Most budgets have footnotes to them, and so, too, does any complete discussion of the budgeting process. One phenomenon that continually confronts the people who budget films is the effect of above-the-line costs on below-the-line costs. Though it might seem that paying a huge salary to a big star would only impact the above-the-line costs, the addition of a marquee name or two has a tremendous ripple effect on the cost of the entire production.

Most big stars have big entourages, whole teams of drivers, bodyguards, even cooks. All of them have to be paid for, as spelled out on the star's contract, but none of their services show up on the screen. Additionally, big stars may only work with certain makeup stylists or hair cutters. The preference of the star for one special makeup artist creates an equation that goes something like this: The star will only work with so-and-so, and knowing this, so-and-so, or his agent, jacks up his asking price accordingly. This kind of off-screen expense can contribute greatly to the negative cost of a film.

Also adding to that negative cost is overhead, a bone of contention between the studios and the producers who make films under their auspices. Since the studios have expenses not directly related to the making of specific films (upkeep of the studio lot, along with such services and facilities as offices, phones, accounting, and other administrative activities), the studios need some special way to reimburse themselves for these expenditures. Most of them call these expenses overhead, and to compensate, they inflate the negative cost of the film by anywhere from 6 to 30 percent, depending on the studio. (Paramount breaks down its services into individually billable items, so it charges no fixed percentage for overhead.)

Obviously, overhead makes it that much harder for films to pay back their cost and then go into profit. Why, some producers ask, should they let the studio's cost of maintaining its sound stages eat into their profits, especially when their own films might have been shot entirely on location? The studios argue that their overhead percentages come very close to what it would cost the production to rent or buy from outside contractors all the facilities and services the studio provides.

Another charge leveled at the studios comes from the independent producers, who claim that a production budgeted at under a million dollars has a way of becoming a multimillion-dollar enterprise at a studio.

"You always have to compare apples to apples," suggests one studio budgeteer. "For instance, when we have an independent producer on the lot making his first film with us, he will generally submit a one-page budget and tell us that's what the film costs. Well, it turns out it isn't what the film will cost at all. He's thinking in terms of nonunion actors and crew, for one example. If we did it his way, with nonunion crews, maybe we could do it for what he estimated. By the same token, he sees quickly that doing it our way, well, it costs what it costs."

Given the unique nature of every film that is produced, and the unique problems that are bound to be encountered during production, the role of insurance is always an important budget line. Without insurance, the entire production is jeopardized by anything from an injured actor to two weeks' worth of shooting ruined through darkroom error. Even the most shoestring independent production usually carries insurance—if only because expensive camera equipment usually cannot be rented without it.

Independents face a host of other problems in budgeting that the studios are able to avoid. The largest of them stems from the fact that independents work within a finite budget. They have raised their funds from a group of friends or investors—or perhaps by successfully submitting a grant proposal. There is no one they can turn to when budget overages begin to occur. They, and their production, are vulnerable to catastrophe literally every moment until the film is finished. Should the indie run out of money halfway through the film, he has wasted a lot of time, money, and hard work.

But even a blue-chip director can encounter a similarly precarious situation. When it became clear that Francis Ford Coppola's *Apocalypse Now* was going to cost $31.5 million—instead of the $12 million that United Artists had budgeted—UA insisted that he serve as the guarantor of the loans they took out to complete the film. Industry observers say that he has paid out more in interest to the bank than the original budget allocated to the film.

Recently, the studios, mini-majors, and independents have all become concerned about a cost that is not reflected directly in the negative cost of a film, a cost that makes it even harder to profit from filmmaking. The amount of money it now takes to promote a film is almost unbelievable.

The film release schedule of 1979 provides a good example, at least statistically, of the dimensions of the dilemma. During 1979 fifty movies were released by the major studios. The combined cost to promote them was estimated by the trade press at around $200 million.

By dividing the number of releases—fifty—into the total promotional outlay on behalf of those releases—$200 million—it appears that the average cost to promote a film in 1979 was around $4 million. (A flop that came out in December of that year, *1941*, cost Columbia some $10 million to promote.) Meanwhile, the average cost to *produce* a film in 1979 was around $5 million. The gap between what it costs to make a film and what it costs to promote a film seems to be getting disturbingly narrow. And the trend continues, distorting the old formula that dictated that a film would go into profit once it grossed three times its negative cost.

It is also a trend major distributors are becoming concerned about. United Artists president Andy Albeck has announced that he is clamping a lid on some of his company's marketing efforts. He notes that UA's earnings on the more than $100 million in total aggregate costs for their films decreased 8 percent in 1979, even though the company had record revenues. Albeck blamed the costs of prints, promotion, and advertising. The effects of these costs are felt even more directly by independents and mini-majors, who can't rely on many of the financing sources available to the major studios.

Many people who are not directly involved in the business of movies —and some who are—often raise the ethical question of whether or not the scores of millions paid in production and promotion for most films today couldn't be better spent on building childrens' hospitals or earmarked for a slate of other socially worthwhile causes. One independent producer has told us that his films have low budgets because he thinks it is "immoral to spend a lot of money on just a film."

The studios recognize this problem, but they also have an answer.

"You can't single us out," says one studio executive. "I mean, should people pay $30,000 to ride around in a car? Hell, no, it's ridiculous. But they do it. Should a movie cost $40 million? I don't know. But they do. After all, we're a business."

6

MAJOR STUDIOS,
MAJOR IMPACT

THE FILM COMPANIES THAT MAKE UP THE MEMBERSHIP OF THE MOTION
Picture Association of America are known in the movie business quite
appropriately as the majors.*

The studios came into existence because the studio system was the
most efficient way to control costs and boost profits. Just as the Industrial Revolution changed a cottage industry, weaving, into an organized, centralized, and managed manufacture in the mills, the studios
imposed a kind of factory system on diverse creative tasks. And, much
like the factory system, there was a great deal of specialization.

In the beginning, stars, besides lending their off-camera exploits to
establishing the idea of Hollywood as the capital of American glamour,
were simply actors, who did not, as many stars do now, produce, direct,
or write the movies in which they played—with the famous exception
of Charlie Chaplin, Douglas Fairbanks, Mary Pickford, and director
D. W. Griffith, who got together in 1919 to found United Artists.
Creative input of the stars was generally limited to tantrums on the

*They are Warner Brothers, Avco-Embassy, Filmways, Paramount, Columbia, 20th
Century-Fox, United Artists, M-G-M, Universal, Disney, and Orion.

set or the threat that they would take a "suspension," or unpaid vacation, from the ironclad contracts that bound them to a specified number of pictures a year for a certain number of years. Even the biggest stars had no real power. They were hired to act, and act efficiently, so as not to send a production into extra days of shooting and added costs. Actors became stars in the first place through a studio apprenticeship program that served to introduce them to the public in small parts at first, in order to test audience acceptance of each new face and figure.

Writers, too, had their specialized function, punching time clocks in writers' buildings, working on made-to-order scripts for the stars. Before the advent of location shooting, production itself was carried out in cavernous sound stages, and each member of the crew had a specialized function to perform—a specialization of talents that unions later fixed forever in place.

During the 1930s and the first half of the 1940s, when the studio system was in full flower, the adaptation of the factory system was paying off. Studios had almost absolute control of their product, making it according to a rigid production schedule with the salaried assistance of skilled specialists. As they do today, studios also saw to the distribution of their product—in those days, they even owned the theaters where their movies played—and tallied the profits.

Like scores of other industries in America, the motion picture business profited greatly from World War II and its aftermath. During the war, when gas rationing was a given, people went to their neighborhood movie houses at least once a week in every city and small town in the country. The government encouraged filmmakers as never before (or since); a weekly diet of "patriotic" pictures was seen as a great propaganda boon to the war effort. It didn't hurt things at the box office, either. After the war a new fact of life, people with money in their pockets to spend, continued the movie boom.

Then, sometime around the late 1940s, the breakup of the studio system began to occur. There are two main historical reasons for this breakup, according to film scholars and armchair historians. The catalyst for the decline seems to have been the "consent decrees," which stripped the studios of the ownership of their theaters following federal suit under monopoly and restraint of trade laws.

The second contributor to a loosening of the hold of the studios was, of course, television. The stew of social, political, economic, and cultural reasons for the rise of television have been amply documented elsewhere, in hundreds of books and articles. From the standpoint of the movie business, what happened was brutally simple: the people in charge of the major studios were too shortsighted to see what the advent of the tube might mean to them in terms of economic opportunity. Somehow forgetting that most of their predecessors had dug in *their* heels at the idea of using the "gimmick" of sound, the studio chieftains felt threatened by television. They called it a passing fad; some of them declared a crusade against television that was supposed to last for twenty years. CBS, RCA, and the other companies engaged primarily in the business of cranking out the new appliance were baffled by the intransigence of the movie moguls. But, being more hardheaded than their counterparts in film, they launched networks of affiliated or wholly owned stations, began to produce their own shows, and found sponsors to pay for it all.

With the wartime shortages of material a thing of the past, television sets began to pop out of the factories and into the homes of people who thought it was just great that this new entertainment medium was "free" once the set was purchased.

(One distribution executive described those days with this colorful analogy: "A movie is like a hooker. You're faced with an inferior product at home, but it's free. That makes it real hard to get your customers to leave the house, even for something they know'll be better." Upon reflection, he admitted that things are still pretty much that way.)

By the mid 1950s, the movie business was on the ropes. It wasn't until the 1960s that the studios began to supply many of the shows that were on television. Today, there are executives at the studios who can still remember the days when only a handful of pictures were made each year at each studio. Faced with the cost of maintaining huge studio plants, the studios also found that those ironclad contracts binding directors, writers, and most especially stars were a double-edged sword. The contract talent had a claim to be paid whether or not movies were being produced. The studios dealt out the money rather than go to court. But, wherever they could, studios began to dismantle the contract system, cut other personnel, sell off the ranches they used for location shooting, and even get rid of pieces of their back lots. (Century City in Los Angeles sits on what used to be a much bigger 20th Century-Fox studio.)

Looking at what once was, compared with what is today, many observers are quick to call the decade or so just before World War II nothing less than the "Golden Age" of the movies. The great stars, the great directors—the great control the studios exercised—seem to characterize this gilded time. By contrast, the studios are seen today as impotent dinosaurs. Actually the truth is a great deal more complicated.

Currently the studios look a lot more like condominium developments than assembly plants. This is the case not only because offices have taken the place of some of the sound stages but because producers are better considered as tenants than as employees. They owe their loyalty in series, that is, to the studio that has them under contract at the moment. Once a producer has moved in at the studio lot, he is more or less free to make his movies the way he sees fit. The studio has thereby gained control over the economic rights to the talents of the producer, but not how those talents are used. In addition, the studio leadership cannot risk alienating the producer in any kind of permanent way. Even though a studio may have only contracted for one movie, it may need that producer again within a couple of years. One final aspect of business, condo style, at the studios: Each tenant keeps to himself, since the good of the individual project rather than the well-being of the studio is uppermost. Under the manufacturing model a director or writer could be switched from one movie to another as consultants to a film that was in trouble. Today, the condominium arrangements at the studios make that kind of pooling of talent unusual.

. . .

Jennings Lang is the only producer left in Hollywood who works directly for his studio, Universal. Given his commercial record in films (*Airport*) and his former position near the top of television production for Universal's parent, MCA, Lang could probably make a deal anywhere. But his position as the last of the breed seems to suit him.

Lang says, "Everybody knows that I get a salary from MCA, not a piece of my pictures. I'm a vice-president of the company, so I want what I do to do well, but I'm here for the long run." He wants MCA to do well, he points out, because he also owns a large block of stock.

Lang lists as the largest attraction of his job something that might startle those producers who claim that the driving force behind their independence is the fear that they will not be free to make their own decisions in another arrangement.

"I can do pretty much what I want here," Lang observes. "If I think we should back a Broadway show, and then hire somebody to direct it or produce it for the screen, I can do it. I don't have to be the producer, I can just pass along the idea. Or if I hear of somebody who might be just right for a picture we're making, I can make the suggestion. People can call on me for ideas or for help every once in a while, too. See, they know I'm not after their job." Of his corporate superiors, he says, "It's the same there. They know I'm doing what I think is going to be best for the company in making pictures. I love what I do. The way I work makes it a lot of fun."

This newly powerful position of the ordinary producer—and in many cases, a hit director, a box office star, or a writer with a brace of commercial successes under his belt—has had an unquestionably significant impact on the studios. It is generally agreed, even at the studios, that the majors no longer serve as the place where film projects are initiated. A script will be brought to a studio for consideration by a producer. Or a producer will ask for money to buy the rights to a best-selling novel, which he will make into a movie under the studio banner. Or a "package" of star, script, and director will be proposed by a producer or, more likely these days, by a powerful agent.

. . .

All of this has given rise to a lot of loose talk about the studios having lost, or somehow willfully abandoned, the creative function. Actually, at the more enlightened studios production executives are often asked for their creative opinions. Most studio executives who are worth their limousines put in endless hours screening unedited film of productions that are in progress. Additionally, it's only fair to accord the studios at least a role as creative accomplice, since once a deal to make a movie is struck at a studio, the entire machinery of that studio is employed in serving the goal of producing that movie.

But if there is relatively little question that the studios have changed from the source of all the production power in the film business to a collaborative role, there isn't much debate, either, over the fact that the studios are still immensely powerful. Their power stems partly from their skill in distributing movies to theaters, at least in this country. We discuss the mechanisms of the distribution chore in a later chapter; for now, it is enough to note that even the most powerful producer needs an efficient organization to get his films to the public and collect the box office receipts.

The real power still enjoyed by the studios can be summed up in one word: money. It is more costly than ever before to mount a production. The rash of film school whiz kids of the 1960s, known at the time for largely low-budget films, need the deep pockets of the studios to finance their creative visions today. George Lucas brought 20th Century-Fox a great deal of fame and fortune with *Star Wars*; Steven Spielberg did the same for Universal with *Jaws* and Columbia with *Close Encounters of the Third Kind.* Francis Ford Coppola made *Apocalypse Now* with the considerable financial help of United Artists.* The hot young independent directors of yesteryear are the hot studio directors of today. Finally, while the demise of the studio system occasioned a rise in the power of the producer to initiate projects, from the standpoint of the studio, it also means that there is no obligation to extend the studio-producer relationship past the current film—

*Recently, he has bought a small studio of his own, Hollywood General.

unless both sides agree to do so. Since few producers enjoy the ongoing patronage of a major studio, all the rest of them spend most of their time looking for a deal that will give them the money they need to make a movie. That's what the current phrase "everybody is an independent producer" really means. It says as much about the position of the producer as it does about the position of the studio: Since the "Golden Age" the power of *both* has adjusted considerably.

Studios get production money from three major sources, not including purchase of stock by relatively small investors. These are, generally: investment by a small group of financiers who specialize in entertainment industry speculation, reinvestment of revenue, and large loans from banks.

Private investment in studio financing is nothing new to the movie business. Producers and studio heads, as a rule, have a select group of large investors they can call on to participate with them in defraying the production costs of future films. The decision on whether or not to call for financing from outside the studio is usually based on a determination that the risks of the production are such that a share in any later profits can be tolerated in exchange for a share of the risks.

Investment and reinvestment of revenue, in the case of a studio owned by a conglomerate, is a matter of the parent company acting as the bank for the production needs of its film division. Where the studio itself owns other concerns, profits can be assigned to the film company in bad box office years and sheltered by losing businesses in years when box office business is good.

Bank loans, too, are a complicated matter, and, as with any other kind of large corporate loan, collateral is required. Sometimes the studio's physical facilities are enough to secure the loan. Otherwise pieces of the profits of several existing films may be put on the line.

"It's like any big loan to anybody," explained an investment counselor who specializes in entertainment financing. "The banks give out, say, $100 million as a line of credit to a studio. That's a loan, and that loan carries with it the requirement that you have to pay interest. Maybe they negotiate it so there's a one-year forgiveness or something, but the studio has to pay that interest. But the bank doesn't want the principal back, not really, just as long as the studio makes the interest payments. If they have a *Star Wars* or something, then they might want it paid down a little, but otherwise, the bank makes a profit on that interest." Interest rates have an impact on studio customers—who borrow at the prime rate in most cases. Studios are always anxious to narrow the time window between the last day of shooting and the first day of release. Even 10-percent interest on a $10 million investment is considerable; studios cannot afford a long waiting time. (Speaking of time, it will be no surprise that the people who run the studios are paid well for theirs. The president of 20th Century-Fox draws an annual paycheck of somewhere around $425,000, not including fringe benefits on a lavish scale demanded by studio executives.)

But it isn't executive salaries or fluctuating interest rates that are drawing attention to the studios on the financial front these days. It's conglomeration, which began a few years ago, when major studios became prime targets for acquisition by cash-rich corporations, whose executives were lured by a combination of the glamour that owning a studio might bring to their roster of companies and by the more essential fact that the losses the studios were then encountering offered opportunities to shelter income from profitable companies owned by the conglomerate. In the second case, such studios themselves, as Universal and 20th Century-Fox began to acquire companies. Some of these acquisitions—film labs, for example—are related to the movie business. Others, such as Coca-Cola bottling plants—a favorite studio acquisition—or the resort facilities of the Aspen Development Corporation, have little to do with film production or distribution. In the third form of conglomeration, film companies already in the stable of such large entertainment corporations as Warners, owned by Warner Communications, found that their contribution to the overall profits of the parent company had dwindled in relation to the profits kicked in by the other members of the corporate team.

In all of these cases, what has happened has been a relative drop in the economic importance of the studio. Either the parent company has lots of other ways in which it makes money besides the studio or the studio has become itself a conglomerate owner, with its film division making less and less difference to the yearly revenue picture.

It is this last feature of conglomeration that appears to be causing concern among some film critics and movie scholars. After their somewhat snobbish dismissal of the new breed of conglomerate executives as people who don't know their projector from their prospectus when it comes to movies—the early film pioneers these same observers revere didn't know anything about movies when they started out, either—the anticonglomerate voices claim that the relatively puny difference made in the profit and loss columns by the studios means that the studios themselves are in jeopardy. In a very good year, they argue, the studio that is part of a conglomerate puts a little under 20 percent in the conglomerate pot. Should the studio have a disastrous year, it is possible that it could be simply dropped, thus erasing from the loss side of the ledger an enterprise that doesn't even make that much of a contribution when it shows a profit.

We may be the only voices among Hollywood writers who think this way, but we can't see anything wrong with conglomeration. The same logic that appealed to the folks who acquired the studios, or diversified the operations of their studios, seems to make sense. Twenty percent is a fairly hefty contribution to profits. And, compared with the expense of making them, films capture a very high share of earnings, which is another way of saying that when films make money, they really make money. The tax advantages of a losing film company hold up under inspection as well. Besides, unlike last year's unsuccessful insurance company, or last season's widgets, last year's films can still make money on television, cable, or even video cassette.

From the standpoint of the film business, conglomeration insures a steady flow of capital to make films through a diversification of risk. The major studios owe their existence to that insurance. Actually, as we will see in the next two chapters, so do the mini-majors and, to some extent, even the independents. A more or less economically stable group of studios, protected from going out of business if one of their films bombs, means that studios can underwrite the bank loans of the mini-majors while they also have enough capital on hand to make deals with the independents.

However, conglomeration nevertheless poses some tough problems for the people who manage the studios. It is imperative that they see themselves and their studios at the beginning of another shift in economic fortune, as profound as that which came with the consent decrees or television. Currently, it looks as though all of the steady money provided by conglomeration has given the studios the freedom to finance a slew of God-awful pictures, apparently without fear of the economic consequences of such a schedule of pure dross. During the next few years, perhaps the studio heads and their corporate masters will see that money also means freedom to experiment, freedom to take a chance with material that is not only commercially but aesthetically viable as well.

7

MINI-MAJORS

SOMEWHERE BETWEEN THE INDEPENDENT PRODUCERS, WHO EXIST from deal to deal, and the major studios, who are assured of a more or less steady flow of corporate cash, is a handful of companies that have attracted a lot of notice in the movie business lately.

They are called mini-majors, or boutique studios, in the trade. Regardless of what name they answer to, these combines that produce or finance films outside the formal studio umbrella are responsible for a growing number of recent box office hits. It's pretty hard to ignore the success of pictures bearing the imprint of Orion Pictures (*10*), Marble Arch (*The Muppet Movie*), Melvin Simon Productions (*Love at First Bite*), or Rastar (*Chapter Two*, *Smokey and the Bandit*).

It's easy to draw the distinction between a mini-major and its larger relations. As one executive at Lorimar (another mini-major) waggishly put it: "The only difference between us and a major is that we don't own any real estate." And, although he was just oiling up a somewhat rusty sense of humor at the time, he did manage to hit the major physical difference between the studios and the minis. Instead of sprawling studio back lots, adding up to acres and acres of land, the minis tend to have as their domain a couple of hundred yards of office space—usually rented office space.

Sharing that office space, which is sometimes situated on a studio lot, are a variety of workers. Foremost are the owners. Unlike studios, with their stockholders and boards of directors, the mini-majors tend to have one, or perhaps a few, highly visible owner-partners. It's their company, and the only review they are subject to is that of the ticket buyers. Although they are all unquestionably businessmen, they tend to immerse themselves in creative matters, something the pared-down structure of the mini-majors lets them do with considerable ease.

The remainder of the mini-major's internal structure is a studio in miniature. Like the studio, the mini-major employs readers, publicists, accountants, lawyers, and even, in some cases, advertising artists, all hired to do close approximations of what they might do at a studio. Only in terms of their numbers is there much difference between them and their studio brethren.

The smallness of these companies is an asset in attracting talent, because deal making seldom gets mired down in a vast bureaucracy. There are fewer hurdles for the prospective film to clear, and the person who makes the ultimate decisions is a little more accessible.

Probably the most important job in the mini-major organization is the fund raiser, who is usually a vice-president. He's the one who goes to the banks, studios, foreign distributors, tax shelter groups, and outside investors in order to get financing for films. It's a job that spans the entire world and isn't really duplicated in the studio model, wherein financial sources are less volatile.

Aside from their lack of real estate and internal structure, the chief characteristic of the minis lies in the fact that they engage exclusively in the production or financing of films. Whereas the studios make movies and get them out to the theaters through a proficient distribution pipeline, the minis make only the films and leave the chore of distribution in this country to the majors, who are the grudgingly acknowledged masters of the trade. (Overseas distribution is another story, discussed in another chapter.) Once this singular character trait of the minis is kept in mind, it's not really too difficult to imagine how the advent of the minis occurred.

Picture makers, whether they were intrigued by deal making or, at the other extreme, obsessed with creative control, would end a late-night grumbling session after a wrangle at one of the studios with: "What do I need these clowns for, anyway? I can make more money, or better pictures, or have more power or fun, on my own. What do I need them for?" The answer that must have come to them was, like everything else in the commerce of celluloid, pretty ambiguous.

On the one hand, location shooting, as we have already noted, means that shooting on a studio lot is no longer necessary. So, the studio lot is only of vestigal importance. Anyway, if a picture needs to be shot on a lot or a sound stage, these facilities can easily be rented.

But making a movie is only half—or less—of the story. The whole point of the exercise, whether one is at heart a dealer or a director, is to get people to come to see the movie one has made. Putting movies on theater screens and patrons in theater seats is done better by the majors than by anybody else. The networks of personal contacts and the stockpile of local lore concerning the preferences of movie house owners and their clientele would take decades to duplicate. The people who built up those connections and logged all of that arcane information could be hired away, but then competition with the studios would ensue, along with a lot of money paid out to distribution experts who would have nothing to do until the first films started to roll.

Then there is the matter of money. Banks could be approached, but it would help the fiscal health of any new venture immensely if the studios would pitch in with some funds in exchange for something *they* might need.

And so on. The point of following the not-so-hypothetical musings of our model filmmaker, worn out from one more tussle with the studio, is that exactly this sort of weighing up of the scene was in fact responsible for the appearance of the mini-majors—and for the shape of their relationship with the major studios.

Related they are—the majors and the minis. All of the minis have distribution agreements in place with major studios. Lorimar has, as they say, inked a pact for fifteen films to be distributed by United Artists.* Orion Pictures and the Ladd Company each have agreements in place with Warners. Rastar has an agreement with Columbia, who recently purchased the company from its leader and founder, Ray Stark. Casablanca had a distribution deal with Columbia, too, prior to its move to Universal—a move unconnected to, but chronologically coincident with, the falling apart of Casablanca's fortunes.

These arrangements, like any good business deal, benefit both parties. The studios, ever hungry for what they are unhappily wont to call product, to feed the appetite of their distribution organizations, get an increased diet of movies to sell—for a cut of the box office gross that usually begins at around 35 percent. The minis, for their part, are assured of giving their movies the best chance of success by using the most efficient method of domestic distribution available. Occasionally, the bargains struck are positively symbiotic, with the studio putting some money into the production pot in exchange for more favorable distribution terms or the chance to distribute the product of the mini-majors on an exclusive basis. (When Alan Ladd, Jr., along with his colleagues Jay Kanter and Gareth Wigan, announced that since running all of the production activities at 20th Century-Fox was becoming a real headache, they had formed the Ladd Company, Warners put considerable financing into the firm in exchange for an exclusive right to distribute the films made by the mini. In a similar way, when the five members of the top management team at United Artists left in a huff over salary and other forms of compensation, they put together Orion Pictures. A $100 million line of credit advanced to this newcomer startled some observers, until it was later revealed that, through a labyrinthine set of contractural subtleties, Warners had agreed essentially to cosign the note. Again, this largesse was granted in exchange for the first crack at domestic distribution of a specified number of Orion films.)

There are exceptions to this general rule. Joseph Wambaugh's Black Marble Films (*The Onion Field, The Black Marble*) was initially

*An agreement that was recently terminated.

financed through the royalties from his books, and the money of his wealthy San Marino, California, neighbors. Wambaugh personally hired and paid the cast and crew for *The Onion Field*. When the film was finished, Wambaugh sold it on a take-it-or-leave-it basis to Avco-Embassy, who also agreed to distribute *The Black Marble*—this time under the more usual pay-for-product setup.

There are other ways to do business as a mini as well. Roger Corman, a man known as King of the B's for his memorable productions such as *Attack of the Crab Monsters*, has an operation that looks like a major studio. Corman finances, produces, and distributes his own product, as well as acts as American distributor for François Truffaut and other foreign favorites. Filmways, too, considers itself a major, and says so in its advertisements to the industry. As for Marble Arch: "We don't consider ourselves a mini at all," huffily observes a spokesman. "We consider ourselves a major studio and we are a major studio. We have a production company [essentially the stateside production arm of Sir Lew Grade's London-based Associated Communications Corporation] and while that means the ever-present need for pictures to release, the nice part is that it's privately owned by Lord Grade." Indeed, often the only way to tell a mini that distributes from a major studio is by the studio's ownership of a back lot.

The fundamental exchange for most of the minis is distribution and/or cash for product. Or, from the perspective of the studios, money in exchange for expertise. It works this way whether the mini in question is Lorimar, with a staff of 600 people during peak film and television production periods; Mel Simon, with a production budget estimated at $100 million this year; or maverick director Robert Altman (*M*A*S*H*, *Nashville*, *A Wedding*, *Popeye*), whose Lion's Gate Films operates out of a renovated brick building in a nondescript neighborhood in West Los Angeles. Altman's business operations make up a fairly clear model of how things stand between the majors and the minis.

According to Lion's Gate president Tommy Thompson, the company takes a script to a major studio in hopes of acquiring the money needed to make the film. In exchange for the money it invests, the studio will distribute the film and share the profits. Altman's skill behind the camera is supposed to be roughly equivalent to the studio's skill in distributing the product. Hence, the rationale for getting together to divide the pie. The deal also allows Altman, as he told us, to make his films exactly the way he wants to make them, under the conditions he wants to make them.

But Altman's control is not actually as complete as he might claim.

In order to see why this is so, we have to back up a bit to examine one of the things that happens when studios undertake to distribute films.

As we will see in a later chapter, matching the movies to the theater in the location that will attract the greatest number of people is the crux of distribution. Doing a good job necessitates all those contacts and all that information at the disposal of the major studios. This sort of a match-up between a given movie, a given theater, and even a certain time of the year (there are supposed to be "Christmas movies" and "summer movies") comes together in what is called the *play date*. A play date can either be good or lousy. Not bad, but lousy. A great film that went nowhere at the box office is said, by the people who made it, to have had a lousy play date. Play dates are fought over, along with the content of the ad campaigns that support them.

The issue of play dates points out just how slippery is the relation between the minis and the majors. An executive at Lion's Gate says that "through a constant stream of information and suggestions, we have about a 30-percent control over how our movies are released." Other sources at other minis also put the figure at somewhere around that mark.

Control of distribution is at the same time control of the fate of the film, whether the filmmaker's goals are primarily artistic or mainly commercial. The studios control distribution. Thus—despite a lot of nonsense written elsewhere lately about the mini-majors bringing a new kind of independence to the movie scene, and due to that independence a new vitality—well, the majors still control the game.

So important is control over the distribution decisions that Eric

Pleskow, president of Orion, told us that in the case of films produced by Orion, he insisted that the distribution mechanism of Warners be placed "totally under our control." In other words, Pleskow demanded, in effect, the right to call the shots at Warners during distribution of his company's product.

Ironically, Orion's only real smash to date, Blake Edwards' *10*, caused a public rift between Edwards and Orion over the advertising campaign for the film. Edwards called it "insulting to the film and to the women's movement." An intriguing twist to the story is the fact that three Pink Panther movies back to back and what Edwards terms "eight movies, of which only one was not a hit," were produced by him at United Artists—for the same folks who now run Orion. Even more interesting, that campaign appears to have helped the film attain $45 million at the box office so far.

Producers yammering at distributors is a common enough occurrence—but usually, the target of invective is a major studio rather than a mini-major. Nor are tempests in trade-paper type the only way in which the more flexible mini-majors are beginning to resemble the majors. Francis Ford Coppola's Omni-Zoetrope (*Apocalypse Now*, *The Black Stallion*) has entered into a production/distribution deal with Orion, itself a mini-major, for a minimum of six movies. Additionally, Coppola recently signed the lease on Hollywood General Studios, where he will establish nothing more or less than his own studio, complete with a planned high school for the performing arts. (The Ladd Company has announced plans to shoot a film on Coppola's back lot.) Other minis have also entered into deals for the services of particular directors for a certain number of films. As a result, the mini-majors may be letting themselves in for the very swamps of administrative detail many of their founders tried to avoid by setting them up in the first place.

Boosters of the mini-majors tend to counter with the argument that the success of the minis only proves that the major studios are abrogating creative decision making even more, relying on the minis to discover new talent and make new films.

That kind of artistic issue can reasonably be argued both ways; the evidence pretty much indicates that the minis and the majors need each other. Indeed, it might be useful to point out that mini-majors are not as much a new and different way of doing business in Hollywood as they are a farm team for the majors. The smaller size of the minis, coupled with easier access to top management—particularly in these days of studio ownership by conglomerates—will probably attract younger, more innovative moviemakers, who will make the "smaller" comedies and love stories that keep the business going and occasionally have a blockbuster among them. Under current deals these are made by the minis but distributed by the majors. Meanwhile, the major studios will continue both to make and distribute the big-league, big-budget science fiction extravaganzas and other garden-variety epics with astronomical price tags—and to supply the back lots and sound stages. Either way, the studios reap revenue from both kinds of movies.

The fact that this is so should come as no real surprise. It serves instead as still another reminder of the fluid nature of arrangements and alliances in the movie business. One year Robert Altman, say, will undertake a rather large studio film, such as *Popeye.* The next year he will hold an informal meeting with his staff, in the converted airplane-seat factory that houses Lion's Gate, and decide to produce and direct a puzzling, personal picture that will make the critics drool and the theater owners groan. The needs of each party—filmmaker, mini, and major—will be reflected in the deal that is eventually struck.

8

INDEPENDENTS

IF AMERICA IS SUPPOSED TO BE THE LAST OUTPOST OF FREE ENTERPRISE,
then the movie business surely must be the last frontier of cowboy
capitalism. In the movies, you can bet on an idea. If it hits, you
supposedly keep a large helping of the profits. If it bombs, you've lost
nobody's money but your own or that of your friends. A lot of people
believe in that ideal, from dentists and doctors who form film financing
syndicates with colleagues to real estate speculators, land developers,
manufacturers, and an occasional rich kid.

Though they are cloaked in obscurity most of the time, they are,
collectively, the people who finance as many as half the films made
each year in the United States. Their movies are not often blockbust-
ers; the majority, in fact, are losers. That's because it's hard to compete
with the studios or mini-majors for the services of the stars and space
on the neighborhood screens. It's harder still when your budget is only
about a third as large as the studios'.

Most of the investors know the odds are tough; if they don't, they
probably have a producer who is part con-man, part monomaniac, to
thank for their ignorance. Still, they put up their money, some with

the devil-may-care attitude of long-shot bettors, others with elaborate formulas for spreading the risk. Apparently, the reward isn't always financial.

In considering the factors that attract outside investors to the film industry, a fine line has to be drawn between them and the rest of the so-called independents. One thing that defines an outsider is that his money has originated in another industry. *Independent* is an umbrella term that covers these outsiders along with many production and distribution companies, and even individual producers. Anyone not affiliated with any of the major studios might be called an independent.

What draws investors to film from other industries? The ones we have chosen to consider each illustrate a different motivation or goal.

"I figured I couldn't lose," said Elsie Wallace, a self-described "fifty-ish" practical nurse who lives in Westchester, California. Though most prospective investors must be hustled, harassed, and cajoled by producers, Mrs. Wallace was eager to invest $5,000—a large share of her savings—in a 1972 film called *Blacksnake,* made by Russ Meyer.

Unfortunately, *Blacksnake* failed to generate either the excitement or the profit margin of such earlier Meyer skin flicks as *The Immoral Mr. Teas* or *Vixen.* A steamy treatment of slavery on a Caribbean island, the film was slated as Meyer's first foray into the black exploitation market, but the movie was never embraced by that—or any other —audience.

As Mrs. Wallace's spirits sank along with her savings, Meyer made an unheard-of move; he gave Mrs. Wallace a small share of the profits of his next film, *Supervixens.* Since then, Mrs. Wallace's investment has been coming back to her in dribs and drabs, but she said she's still a little short of the break-even point.

The size and circumstance of Mrs. Wallace's investment may be at the opposite end of the spectrum from the deals made by investors who are drawn to films to round out a portfolio of more conservative ventures. But their motives are the same. Investors in films who risk a lot or a little are gambling on the potential of spectacular profits. Insiders call it the home run syndrome.

"A lot of people look on movies as risky," observed Bill Harvey, a real estate developer from Dallas who also owns part of the Texas Rangers baseball team.

"I made my first money with dinner theaters, had a chain of them, the Windmill Theaters in Houston, Dallas and Fort Worth, and Phoenix. There's more bankruptcy in theaters and restaurants alone than just about any other business. When you put them together, I guess your odds are unbelievable. But I made money."

Harvey, who put "under $25,000" into a mid-1970s Roy Rogers movie called *MacIntosh and T.J.*, explained, "I'm an active guy. I didn't invest for tax shelters, I've got enough in the real estate business. I bet on the film, I bet on the people. I wanted to make money."

He has yet to do that, even though the film he helped back has received some distribution. In late 1979 Harvey said that he had heard from the film's Los Angeles–based producer, and had been told that "there was a chance" the investors would get their money back.

The producer, Tim Penland, a born-again Christian whose Penland Productions makes documentaries for the Baptist Radio and Television Network and television commercials for Radio Shack, put together the deal for *MacIntosh* along a kind of Oklahoma-Texas axis. Friends told friends or one lawyer talked to another, and so on.

"I had a lot of investors from west Texas on my picture," he said. "We had a barbeque scene in the picture and they all came to the party to be in the film. They loved to sit around and be a part of it."

Penland admitted to being disappointed in the take of his first theatrical film, but he continues to try to get other deals rolling. His business letterhead still carries the legend "Producers of *MacIntosh and T.J.*"

Penland continued: "A year or so ago, if you'd have asked me if Harvey will get his money, I would have just said it was a write-off and that's it. Now it looks really good. Columbia is handling pay TV distribution for us and we are working on some foreign sales." Penland pointed out, though, that Harvey will have to wait a while longer for the cash to begin to flow. "He won't see any money next year or anything," Penland explained. "Columbia has the picture for twenty years. But I'd say that over the next seven to ten years, it will total up to a nice return. . . . Remember, in essence he's already gotten back half the money from the tax savings."

Still open to film investing, Bill Harvey has listened to a pitch from a group of entrepreneurs who were looking for cash to build a combination film and recording studio in Dallas. He was interested, but the people involved never called him back.

In 1976 a group of L.A. businessmen bet on what they must have thought was a sure thing. It was a film called *Slithis,* about a monster that rises from the sludge of the canals in Venice, California. As subject matter, horror is the closest thing to a safe bet that exists in the film business. But something else about the film made it seem even more appealing to the investors: It would be made for only $100,000, an amount which should have been fairly easy to recoup.

There's no longer any set formula to determine what percentage of the gate will eventually fall into the hands of the producer. Out of every admission dollar, the theater owner must first deduct his expenses; he also keeps a previously agreed-upon percentage. With major studio films, the percentage retained by the theater owner can be as low as 10; with *Slithis* it varied from 75 to 85. That was because such independents as the producer and distributor of *Slithis* don't have much leverage with the theater owners; they don't have other films coming up that the theater owners desperately want.

Once the theater owners eat up their percentages, the rest of the money then goes to the distributor, who also takes out overhead (the cost of prints, promotion, and advertising) and pays regional subdistributors who handle the film across the country. What is left goes to the producer, who must pay back his investors before he can pocket a profit.

All these figures lead independent producers to the realization that for every dollar spent in production, they must earn ten or twelve dollars at the box office to see any sort of profit. Thus, the less they spend, the better chance they have of turning a profit. Unfortunately for many investors, this equation doesn't always work. *Slithis* grossed at least $2.4 million, but neither the producer nor any of the investors have yet seen even a penny of profit.

The producer of *Slithis* is Stephen Traxler, a former actor and Vietnam veteran. He said that he gathered the investors in his film together "like a Tupperware party. I met one guy on a diving trip to Catalina and he told other people." Traxler's contacts supplied about half the money needed to make his film. The other half of the budget came from a Nebraska theater owner and distributor named Dick Davis. Davis also served as the distributor for *Slithis*, an arrangement that is fairly typical in the world of independent production. In return for his investment of around $50,000, Davis secured distribution rights as well as a percentage of the profits. Thus, he stood to make money two ways if *Slithis* was a success.

Recalling the summer of 1979, Traxler reported, "The film did fairly well here in L.A. last summer, but I didn't think the subdistributors out here really did enough. We had *Slithis* survival kits and *Slithis* fan club cards all over the rest of the country. It worked real well, but none of that happened out here." Traxler also claimed that in many theaters posters advertising the film as a coming attraction never arrived. "Now if I had to put blame, I would put it on Davis," Traxler said.

The young producer had another complaint as well: "I really can't say how the film has done, because Davis won't show us any of the books. We have a contract that stipulates that we receive a full accounting of all monies. To this date, we have yet to see any books."

Davis for his part seemed unimpressed with Traxler's charges.

"I feel bad that Steve and I are having this problem," Davis said. "He has seen some books, definitely. But he's got to realize that I haven't even gotten back my distribution costs yet and I've got about $75,000 of my own money tied up in this.

"Steve's problem is that he's a good filmmaker who doesn't understand distribution. I made three trips out to L.A. to look after his film, and my subdistributors were people who did *Halloween* and *Harper Valley P.T.A.* They know what they're doing," Davis declared.

"I could tell everybody right now the right way to do this or that," Traxler sighed. "But if you want to make your first film and get it out, you'll make a deal with the devil."

. . .

Some investors get into film almost by accident. A realtor in Burbank, California, was feuding with the IRS on the question of his tax liability for a collection of personal real estate deals.

The realtor, who asked that his name not be used, won his case, but he was left with the feeling that diversification was the best way of preventing more wrangles with the feds. A tenant in a building he owned had just landed a job with producer Patrick Curtis, known for the profitable *Kansas City Bomber*, featuring his ex-wife, Raquel Welch. The tenant brought the realtor and Curtis together.

A soft-spoken, slightly built man in his early fifties who spends his days working in a storefront office, the realtor described himself as "not a big filmgoer." But as a boy in Connecticut he used to shine shoes in order to scrape together the price of admission to Saturday afternoon serials. The film he bought into is a compilation of those serials, spliced together and spiced up by dialogue from Phil Proctor and Peter Bergman of the Firesign Theater. The realtor bet $200,000, about 30 percent of his savings, he said, that the nostalgia value of the serials would return his investment, along with a sizable profit. He must have reasoned that his investment had a fairly good chance because of the film's low, $400,000 budget and the degree of cost control that came with the fact that most of the footage for the movie had been shot during the 1930s and 1940s.

He was wrong. The film, *The Day the Earth Got Stoned*, was completed in late 1978 under the title *The Secret World War* and has yet to see any meaningful distribution. Bergman has said that the film would appeal to the same audience that made *The Groove Tube* and *Kentucky Fried Movie* hits, adding that he and Proctor had something they called "complete rational control" over the project. If it failed, they said, it would be their fault.

That's little comfort to the Burbank realtor, who now feels that he has little chance of recouping any of his investment.

Once into production, problems developed. The other half of Curtis's financing fell through, but he elected to struggle ahead using just the realtor's money. Production expenses piled up, too, with the editing and writing taking longer than expected.

Eventually, Curtis realized that he would need more money in order to complete the film. He made a deal with William Howard, who owns a travel agency as well as business interests in Europe. Representing his Virgin Islands–based film distribution company, Amphibian Ltd., Howard promised Curtis a total of $125,000 in exchange for foreign distribution rights to the film, which at that time was going under still another name, *J-Men Forever*. Curtis and the realtor agreed to the deal, giving up all future interest in the foreign earnings of the film. This move limited the realtor's earning potential on the movie, but he was compensated by a larger share of the hoped-for domestic distribution income.

A little later, though, Curtis entered into another agreement with Howard. This one, which the realtor did not sign, modified the first contract, carrying the stipulation that if Curtis didn't finish the film on time, *all* rights to it would go to Howard. Curtis got out of this second contract a greater percentage (66 percent) of Howard's $125,-000 to be paid to him immediately. Unfortunately for Curtis and the realtor, the film was not completed within the specified time and Howard confiscated the film. He later made a deal with a New York company, International Harmony, to distribute.

Recalling his contract with Howard, Curtis said he wagered only the 50% share his company, Curtco, had in the film. He insisted that the realtor's interests were "not in jeopardy." Bill Howard didn't see it that way. "I have the negative and I have the copyright," Howard said, adding that if the realtor had any grievances, he should take them up with Curtis. Howard's view was that any returns from the film would go to him exclusively.

But what was Howard thinking when he entered into an arrangement he knew might leave the principal investor in the movie high and dry?

"To tell you the truth," Howard said, "that was so long ago, and there's been so much happening since, I don't remember what I thought about that." He repeated, though, that the matter is legally "between the realtor and Patrick."

Curtis eventually came to believe, somewhat petulantly, that Howard was "one of those people who try to run other people's lives by being clever." He indicated that he felt Howard's extensive claims on the film would not hold up in court, although to date there has been no legal test. "Why bother?" Curtis asked. "The film hasn't made any money."

At the core of the realtor's complaint is his belief that the film would have been a winner but that ownership hassles prevented it from being released at that special moment when the public was ready for it. Neither Curtis nor Howard agreed with that assessment of the film's commercial potential.

In defending himself, Curtis cited a combination of personal problems and the intense pressure he felt to finish the film, no matter what. In the wake of its completion Curtis led a nomadic existence. The realtor couldn't locate him, and when asked directly for a phone number, Curtis gave that of the L.A. *Playboy* mansion.

Happily for the realtor, the loss of $200,000 didn't exactly send him to the poorhouse. Unlike some investors, though, he didn't immediately use his failed investment as a tax write-off. "That would be saying the film is a total loss, and I don't believe that," he commented. Ultimately, he has decided the reason things went so badly for him is that he made the mistake of just sitting back and watching instead of actively involving himself in the decision making.

"I lost control," he concluded glumly.

In 1976 John Jurgens, heir to the Jurgens Lotion Company fortune, bought an option on Hunter S. Thompson's *Fear and Loathing in Las Vegas.* The book, a drug-crazed account of a convention of narcotics agents, made the author's reputation and, thanks to being serialized in *Rolling Stone,* was exposed to a huge, admiring audience. John Jurgens, then in his twenties, was one of those admirers. He had begun his involvement in film by helping to finance the completion of a ski documentary called *Winter Equinox.* Skiing had been an enthusiasm of Jurgens's and that had led him to the documentary. Now *Fear and Loathing* had become another of his enthusiasms.

After optioning the book Jurgens and the producer he hired, Michael O'Connor, commissioned writer Larry McMurtry (*The Last Picture Show*) to turn Thompson's book into a screenplay. Meanwhile, Jurgens and O'Connor set out to drum up interest for the project at studios and with actors and directors. What everyone thought would be a hot project moldered on the shelf for years.

Jurgens has always maintained that he could finance the film out of his own money but agrees that the scope of the production would be less limited if it were financed by a studio.

So, O'Connor made the rounds of the studios. He was either turned down or put on indefinite hold. One studio observer of O'Connor's travails later noted that even though the property had a lot of public recognition, there are some things a studio won't do in order to cash in on that potential. One of them seems to be entrusting millions of dollars in production money to untried producers.

At Universal a producer who did have a track record, Art Linson (*Carwash*), was able to get a Hunter S. Thompson movie off the ground. Also acting as director, Linson finished *Where the Buffalo Roam* in 1980, only to have it panned by the critics and bomb at the box office. Early on, Linson had offered to buy just the title *Fear and Loathing* from O'Connor and Jurgens, but they wouldn't sell, still certain that they would eventually get their own film off the ground.

After the failure of *Buffalo,* Jurgens and O'Connor were still optimistic about their own chances. "Anything that gets the Thompson name before the public is good," O'Connor added, in reference to *Buffalo's* ad compaign.

When last encountered, Jurgens was considering enrolling in law school—something he'd been thinking about for at least the preceding year and a half. O'Connor was expecting a decision from a studio vice-president, something he'd been doing for just as long. The one lesson they said they'd learned is that Hollywood deal making often moves at a glacial pace. Their main holdup was with director Martin Scorsese (*Mean Streets*, *Taxi Driver*), who expressed a desire to direct

Fear and Loathing but whose attention was taken up time and again by other assignments. At least one other director has come and gone since Scorsese, and so have a handful of interested actors.

It's a long jump from the nominal film involvement of an investor such as John Jurgens to the $100 million movie plunge taken by the huge A. E. Guinness Co., Limited, of England. But somewhere in the corporate labyrinth there's surely someone who shares Jurgens's attraction to the medium. Big companies don't commit millions of dollars (or pounds sterling) because somebody in the hierarchy is "into film," though; Guinness's official reasons were practical enough so that anyone in a three-piece suit could understand them.

By 1977 Guinness had saturated its North American market. Everyone who was going to buy Guinness beer was already buying it; there was no more room for growth. The answer appeared to be diversification, but to what? Film offered the benefit of name identification ("The Guinness Group presents . . .") and it also had a convincing advocate in the person of Richard St. Johns.

The son of Adela Rogers St. Johns, Richard St. Johns had been an independent producer and movie company executive. A friend of his, an attorney in San Francisco, did the matchmaking that brought St. Johns and Guinness together.

Guinness began by taking a minority financial interest in some of St. Johns's productions. The films, *Matilda, Circle of Iron,* and *Nightwing*, were all losers, but that didn't stop Guinness from pumping still more money into the company. An insider noted that although the first films didn't do well at the box office, distribution guarantees, TV sales, and tax benefits were enough to keep Guinness from losing its interest in the film business.

In addition to a production slate of eight new movies—including *A Change of Seasons* with Bo Derek, Shirley MacLaine, and Anthony Hopkins—Guinness also owns Producers Sales Organization. PSO handles foreign distribution rights of more than ten films a year, for Guinness and for other movie companies.

St. Johns, whose new title is managing director, points out: "Guinness is in the film business to stay. It's not a short-term deal, from picture to picture. We're just like Warners."

And St. Johns offered a reason for outside investors making a first plunge into the film business: "It's more fun than the steel business or real estate. There are no fun guys in real estate. And if there are, they eventually get into films."

Another potent attraction of film investing to outsiders is the challenge. Many of the investors are successful, self-made men, just the kind of people who have spent lifetimes applying workaholic temperaments to successfully overcoming immense obstacles in a variety of different businesses.

The Manitou, a rather unsuccessful horror film starring Tony Curtis, was backed in part by Herman Weist, who "wanted to expand my field of endeavor, get into something new." Weist piled up a fortune in the electronics industry, adding more income with the development of a machine that makes plastic bags. After two decades of involvement with his own firms, Weist was introduced to films by two friends, Mel Gordy and the late William Girdler, Jr. Girdler, who died in January 1978 in a helicopter crash while scouting movie locations in the Philippines, had directed a number of low-budget films—among them *Grizzly.* Girdler matched his talents with producer Gordy on *The Manitou* and invited Weist to invest.

Weist, who lives on the Ohio River near Louisville on an eighty-five-foot yacht complete with helicopter pad, was initially undaunted by the failure of *The Manitou.* He was in the planning stages for two other films, but even then, in mid 1978, Weist had his doubts about the film business.

"The film business is foreign to the way I usually do business," he said. "I started my corporations from scratch and ruled the plants with an iron thumb. In film, different people are the kings of their fields . . . I was used to dealing eye to eye, shoulder to shoulder with people, but out there [Hollywood], it's specialized. It's a mammoth job."

Within a year, Weist was out of movies. The doubts he initially expressed about the movieland style of doing business eventually became the reasons for his departure. Specifically, he objected to having to go to other sources for money. Weists's deals with Gordy were set up so that Weist would supply only development money. Once that money had gone toward a script and securing a distribution deal, other investors became involved. Weist wasn't comfortable with that. "I prefer to use my own money," he said. "I won't say I'm disappointed. I'm not happy with it. That's about all I can say."

One of the most intriguing reasons for investing in movies is a positive belief in the message that shows up on the screen. In those cases—rare as they are—the investment becomes a contribution, a method of film financing that is virtually unheard of in Hollywood.

"Economically, Hollywood is not the center of the universe. It's just a tiny speck in terms of the gross national product," according to Robert Munger, executive producer of the film version of Charles Colson's book, *Born Again*. Munger, himself a born-again Christian, claimed that he had more prospective investors than he needed on the film of the one-time Nixon hatchet man's post-Watergate religious experiences.

"The people I know could buy the Burbank Studios and move it to Santa Monica with their petty cash. They have a personal net worth of $5 or $10 *billion*. But," he noted, "these are people who regular people in Hollywood don't know about. They're conservative Republicans. The people who control the studios are left, liberal. These investors are not going to put out money to have Jane Fonda in a movie that says the U.S. is terrible and Russia is great."

One of Munger's born-again Christian investors was Clayton Brown, a Chicago investment counselor specializing in tax exempt state and municipal bonds. He said that he and his partner, Tony Wauterlek, helped back *Born Again* with $150,000 of their own money because "we wanted to get the message across through the film medium."

"I'm not a crusader," Brown said. "Films are a far cry from the investments we usually make. As an individual and a parent, I would like to see less pornography and violence, but to single out one industry for reform is going too far.

"We were so impressed with Chuck Colson and his testimony and witness of the prison ministry that we invested as a donation to that. We really don't need any more material gain."

Prior to the film's release Munger spoke of the "70 million born-again Christians out there who want a film they can relate to." But after the film had been out for a year, a spokesman for the distributor, Avco-Embassy, said sourly that the film's dismal grosses "only go to show that none of those people go to the movies."

From his Chicago office Brown said, "Sure, to be perfectly honest, I am a little disappointed. But that doesn't change the nature of the investment for me."

Brown received a little more than $32,000 from the movie, all of which he says he donated to Colson's Prison Fellowship program. He was annoyed not at the loss of any revenue he might have realized, but rather that "more people didn't get to see the film."

"We had a premiere here in Chicago for the movie, with the Prison Fellowship to be the main beneficiaries. It was very successful, and afterwards people asked when they could see the film here in town at a theater. Well, Avco never opened it at a commercial theater."

Surprisingly undaunted, Brown concluded, "If a film struck me the same way that this one did, I would invest in it."

If Clayton Brown's serene approach to taking a flyer in films makes him a special case, it's important to keep in mind that independent production in the 1980s will probably become a rather special case itself.

After the new age of independent production peaked two or three years ago, independent films have been rapidly eclipsed by the big money releases of the studios or the new combinations of mini-majors.

Some independents claim that studio production and the output of the minis—for the most part distributed by the studios—are crowding them off the screens.

Roger Corman, whose low-budget classics such as *The Little Shop of Horrors* and a string of motorcycle pictures that gave a start to Peter Bogdanovich, Francis Ford Coppola, Jack Nicholson, and literally a score of others, laments: "The days when a kid comes out of the hills with a great $100,000 film are over."

Mark Tenser, president of Crown International Pictures, has said, "We have seen a market completely dominated by the major studios and their superpictures. . . . There is a tendency in prosperous times to forget those who were there when you needed them," Tenser warns theater owners. "Many exhibitors have forgotten." Citing decreasing screen opportunities for independents, Tenser has gone on to note that many independents have abandoned theatrical films in favor of either television or cable television production. "There is a danger here which could point us into markets that would minimize our exposure and lessen our gamble. . . . Who will then give young, talented people a chance?" he asks.

Compared with most independents, Corman and Tenser speak from a privileged perspective. The plain truth is that most independent, low-budget productions are doomed to indifferent distribution, delays between payday and play date that can sag into years, and income reports that are either sketchy or hard to verify. The independents who stay in business—Corman's New World Pictures, Crown, Cannon, Guinness, American Cinema Releasing, Film Ventures International, and others—make distribution deals with the major studios, reorganize as mini-majors, do business as high-risk concerns fueled by a stable pool of savvy investors, or combine these strategies in order to survive.

The lone entrepreneur equipped with an idea and a passion to see it made into a film is fast becoming a vanishing breed on the last frontier of private enterprise, Hollywood style.

9

TAX SHELTERS:

EVERY CITIZEN
A MOGUL?

"I CALL IT THE PIG SYNDROME," SAYS THE MAN FROM PRICE WATER-house & Company, accountants. In his Century City office, overlooking the placid greenery of the Los Angeles Country Club, Burt Forester has been trying to explain why motion picture tax shelter laws tend to be short-lived. His opinion is a rare instance of bluntness in what is otherwise the confusing and rather dry business of U.S. and foreign tax shelters for films.

Tax sheltering for the movies is a game of loopholes and legal interpretations, a pursuit that is more an art than a science.

The basic anomaly—and attraction—in tax shelters is that they usually let you say you lost more income on a business deal than you really have lost. This, in turn, usually means that at tax time you get to keep more of your income than you would have kept if you had not bought into the tax shelter. In general, tax shelters are designed for the short run; take a big loss now and cut your taxes, but be prepared in future years to accept your gains, if there are any. You're betting that your future income will be lower and you will be better able to absorb the gain.

Forester described a tax shelter investment of his own: "This year [1980] I invested $350 in low-cost housing. Next year, I'll have to invest substantially more, but for this first year, on an investment of only $350, my tax savings will be about $2,500."

Forester defends deals such as this by pointing out that the government gives a tax break to people who support worthwhile projects—low-cost housing, for example. But does our government think that moviemaking is a worthwhile endeavor, to be encouraged by allowing for tax shelters? Apparently not. According to Forester and other observers, U.S. tax laws tend to give a break to businesses that involve heavy financial risks, and though movies are among those businesses, the laws were probably not made with movies in mind. However, when the tax laws were changed in 1976—a move that ended half a dozen years of motion picture tax shelters in the U.S.—the film business was most definitely considered by the legislators. In effect, they told Hollywood to look elsewhere for production money.

In the United States before 1976 there were two kinds of movie tax shelters, one called the "purchase" shelter and one called the "production service company." What first has to be understood about film investing—as it worked then and now—is that if you have a yearly income of $100,000 and spend all of it in one year to get a movie made, you still owe the IRS a tax (a sizable one) on that $100,000. (In England, as this is written, new tax laws have declared that there would be no tax liability in this model situation. Not too surprisingly, American producers began a stampede to England in search of financing.) In this country money invested in film has always been considered to be the purchase of an asset. However, some investors find that a loss can be a kind of asset . . . if the loss can be purchased for less than face value.

This brings us to the purchase tax shelter. The way those usually worked was that somewhere, often in Europe, a producer would make a film for very little money. It sat on a shelf in a vault somewhere because it was terrible. But along would come a syndicate of American investors offering the producer money for his film. Let's say the film cost $200,000 to make. The investors, five in number, perhaps doctors, lawyers, dentists, or other professionals with high salaries and low business expenses, would offer the producer, say, $800,000 for his film. That amount is much greater than the film's cost, but not, necessarily, its *worth*, since any movie could be worth much more at the box office than it cost to make. Hence, the investors could reason, it is fair to pay an inflated price. But when it actually comes time to pay that price, the investors would only give the producer $250,000 in cash and $550,000 worth of IOU's, a particular sort of IOU called nonrecourse notes.

Technically, the investors—now the new owners of the film—were telling the producer—the former owner—that once the movie started making money, they would make good on their $550,000 worth of IOUs. But if the movie never made any money, then the producer would never be paid the rest of his money. The investor's debt to him would be canceled, and the producer would have no recourse. He couldn't put a lien on the investor's property or do any of the other things that are done when one person owes another person money.

What was in it for the producer? He got a movie made and his costs back. But what about the investors? Why would they bother to inflate the price of the film? For them, there were enormous tax benefits in those nonrecourse notes. Since, technically, they were risking money by going into "debt" to the producers, they could write off the sum of the cash they invested *plus* the face value of the nonrecourse notes, if the film flopped. Thus, for tax purposes, they could say they had lost considerably more money than they had actually taken out of their pockets. Later, the amount of the nonrecourse notes would show up as *income* on the investor's tax return, since a canceled debt is basically the same thing as income. But due to income-averaging rules and other delaying tactics, this transition could be put off for years. When it finally occurs, the hunt will be on for new tax shelters.

Asked why the IRS would allow a person to declare he was risking money he wasn't, Burt Forester simply says that real estate works that way, and the movie tax shelters were based on the real estate model. But why should that practice be allowed in real estate? "Because they have a big lobby," Forester says.

In the other tax shelter model, the production service company, the workings were geared more toward films that had a good chance of being successful. It had to be that way in order to convince the banks to help in their financing.

Under normal circumstances a private investor would put up some of his own money and a much larger chunk of money borrowed from a bank. The bank loan was a nonrecourse arrangement—it would be paid back only out of money made by the film. But the investor could say he invested, and was at risk for, the sum of the out-of-pocket cash plus the loan. To get the loan the investor had to be a good customer of the bank, and the bank had to be convinced that the project had the elements to make it a success. *Shampoo*, with Warren Beatty, and *The Great Gatsby*, with Robert Redford, were both financed this way.

The investors would then contract a production service company to make the film, and after it was made, the film would be sold to a studio for money that would be deferred—paid later—out of the film's earnings.

Finally, the investor would get what he wanted: an immediate tax loss, for *that year*. After all, the film hadn't even been released yet, so it couldn't have made any money. Once the dollars started rolling in during the succeeding years, it would be time for another tax shelter.

The production company would not have shared in the profits but would, of course, have been paid a fee for its services.

The reader who is beginning to develop a hankering to hand out some of those nonrecourse notes to his friends and relatives would do well to remember that nonrecourse financing of movies is no longer allowed. Furthermore, even in the days when it was, the IRS was not wholly approving; according to Burt Forester, over two hundred movie tax shelter cases from the pre-1977 era are still pending before the tax courts.

Looking back at the tax shelter years in the United States, there's little cause for nostalgia. True, they were a stimulant to the industry. They helped keep crews and talent working. They gave first breaks to a few people. And they even caused a few good films to be made. But when Congress got an indication of the tax money being channeled away from the IRS, as well as the abuses being perpetrated, it voted their demise.

That goes back to Burt Forester's pig syndrome. As he sees it, the tax game is not one of hard and fast rules but, rather, give and take. Set up a shelter to give yourself a comfortable advantage, not a gigantic one, Forester advises. Otherwise you'll poison the well for everyone. Awful films were made just to take advantage of the law. Outrageous write-offs were not uncommon. People entered ventures with the hope of losing money. It really couldn't have lasted.

What has lasted in the United States are accelerated depreciation for movies and an investment tax credit. Depreciation is money deducted from taxes to make up for wear and tear on business assets. In film the investor is allowed to deduct a lot very quickly, since film tends to be a very perishable commodity. Six months to two years in the marketplace, and a film has lost almost all of its earning potential. This is true for the most successful films as well as for the losers. So the government makes a generous allowance for depreciation.

There is a complicated and disputed formula for figuring out the exact amount of depreciation. It involves estimating the future earnings of the film and comparing them, in the form of a fraction, with the film's actual income. Accelerated depreciation was also the centerpiece of the tax shelters. Nonrecourse notes merely inflated the amount of the investment; accelerated depreciation meant that that investment could be written off in its entirety much more quickly than a normal investment. Often, the quick giant losses that this figuring gave investors were spread out over several years, to maximize the tax advantages.

Another break the U.S. government gives investors is an investment tax credit of 6 1/2 percent. This means that a movie investor can immediately deduct 6 1/2 percent of his investment from his income for tax purposes.

Though that's no big deal, it should be recalled that the U.S. government is the world's largest producer of films—not commercial features but educational and industrial films, which through sheer volume offer a lot of work to filmmakers. Though relatively few Hollywooders take this avenue, these do constitute opportunities to help filmmakers from other parts of the country, both in terms of income and learning experience. Still, for many in Hollywood, this major involvement is virtually meaningless. So American filmmakers now look to other countries for help in financing.

As the American tax shelter money was vanishing in 1976, Germany suddenly became a new source of funding—for American as well as German films. In the view of many, German tax laws were more hospitable to sheltering due to a German government plan to encourage the cinema business in that country. Germany's Ufa studios had been fertile ground for the development of movie talent in the 1920s, but the rise of Nazism sent most of that talent packing to Hollywood. The native German cinema was slow to recover.

Finally, in the mid 1970s, such filmmakers as R. W. Fassbinder and Werner Herzog helped recapture some critical attention for the German cinema. Observers agree that tax shelter money helped create a climate favorable to new talent in that country. This money also helped the American cinema.

It's not known whether the German lawmakers expected German citizens to invest in American movies, but they should have had at least an inkling. After all, American films—Hollywood movies—are generally accepted in Western countries as the big league. Western Europeans would have little trouble recognizing America's top ten box office draws, but it would be just about impossible for an average American to name even one actor working in Germany. As a result, American movies tend to be a form of international currency—good in almost every country. Further, they're also exploitable in the single largest market, the United States itself. The same can't be said about very many non-American films. As a result, German investors looked to the American cinema as a place to put their money.

Naturally, this was not a move that pleased the general populace of Germany, who perceived rich people taking their money out of the country to avoid taxes. It was the kind of bad publicity that can kill a tax shelter law. Some American filmmakers, in need of funding, found their way around this potential problem. Geria, a German company that collected money from Germans and then invested it in tax shelters, helped finance a number of "American" films. The quotation marks are used because the issue of nationality is slightly blurred. Such films as *Fedora, Bloodline, Twilight's Last Gleaming,* and *Who's Killing the Great Chefs of Europe?* were conceived and guided through production by Americans, but locales and crew were often German. It's important to note that German law did not require this. David Picker, an American consultant to Geria at that time, claimed that the policy was only that of Geria and that it was conceived as a way of avoiding a public outcry in Germany.

Other German companies haven't emulated Geria's patriotism—or its sense of public relations. *Being There,* American in both ownership and outlook and shot entirely in the United States, was partially funded by a German tax shelter company called Cip. So were two other profoundly American movies, *Hair,* and *Americathon.*

Lorimar, the American mini-major, helped open the way to German money with *Twilight's Last Gleaming,* and continued a heavy involvement with German money through *Americathon, Great Chefs,* and *Being There.* The company's executive vice-president, Jack Schwartzman, is an expert on the foreign tax shelter situation.

By late 1979, according to Schwartzman, German money had all but stopped flowing, a situation Schwartzman attributes to the abuses that always crop up in tax shelter schemes. He cites Lorimar's and others' efforts to make "quality" films while still others were content to crank out anything just for the tax benefits. Currently, Schwartzman hopes to arrange tax shelter financing of Lorimar films with investors in England, Australia, South Africa, Austria, and Japan. "Why are we doing this?" Schwartzman asks, and then answers his own question: "Go to the Federal Reserve Bank. We need the least expensive financing we can get, and we don't have that with their interest rate." Whatever the fluctuations of the prime rate, Schwartzman will no doubt continue searching for new, untapped sources.

Meanwhile, Lorimar has finished its final deal with Cip and has lost touch with Geria. Geria's one-time consultant, David Picker, didn't lose touch with Lorimar, though. In March 1980 his office was at Lorimar, right next to Jack Schwartzman's.

Schwartzman's comments on tax shelters also lead to an added insight. Though agreeing that the film industry is beneficial to the U.S. economy because it is a net exporter rather than importer, Schwartzman points out that lots of other industries perform that same function. So why do movies deserve a special break? he asks. An answer to that question, one that Schwartzman has apparently not considered, is that movies are an art form in addition to being a commercial venture. Film can be the most powerful and immediate of the art forms, when used properly, and also the most far-reaching. Do governments have an obligation to support art in general, and film in particular? This question is at the bottom of the tax shelter issue, and it's something to consider.

Presently, the U.S. government seems to view film as just a business. The Small Business Administration likes to see businesses of all kinds bloom, because that means more tax dollars flowing into the treasury. Shortly after Congress stopped most movie tax shelters, a group of lawyers approached the Small Business Administration with an interesting plan. These lawyers, some of whom had been involved in forming tax shelter deals, now wanted the SBA to help finance movies.

One of these lawyers was Norbert Simmons, who later went on to head a company called MCA–New Ventures. Simmons helped pioneer the use of government money in filmmaking through his fundraising efforts for *The Black Godfather* and *The River Niger.* To get financing for both of these films, Simmons went to Minority Enterprise Small Business Investment Corporations (MESBICs). MESBICs are essentially investment companies funded partially by the government and partially by private concerns. Although the MESBICs Simmons contacted had not previously been involved in film, it was generally agreed that it was within their charters to help finance films made by and for black people. With those two projects under his belt, Simmons joined a group of lawyers who were talking to the Small Business Administration about setting up Small Business Investment Corporations (SBICs) that would deal exclusively in film.

Movie MESBICs and movie SBICs function in the same way—only

the concern for minority groups separates the former from the latter. To simplify a process of years into a few sentences, we offer the following explanation of how a Small Business Investment Corporation works: An entrepreneur contacts the Small Business Administration and suggests that, say, minority involvement in filmmaking needs to be encouraged. The SBA then analyzes that suggestion from the social and economic points of view.

In the event that consideration of these points yields a favorable opinion, the SBA licenses an MESBIC or SBIC. But the cash will not yet flow. First, the MESBIC or SBIC has to raise and then invest a designated amount of money from private sources. This amount can be as much as $5 million, and only when all of it has been invested can government money begin to be spent. At this point, the SBA quadruples whatever the MESBIC or SBIC has gotten from other sources.

The advantages of this arrangement are obvious. For a cash outlay of $1 million the MESBIC partners can make four times that in investments. True, the government's money must eventually be repaid, but the terms are easy. The government's money is considered to be a low-interest loan, which comes due in ten years. On any films produced, the MESBICs and SBICs share in the profits. It also means that as investors, the MESBICs and SBICs run the standard risk of losing their entire investment. That's where another of the SBA's easy terms comes in handy. Should a MESBIC or SBIC come up short after ten years, the SBA has the power to offer an extension of the loan or forgive it. This provision relates to the idea of the government supporting the social purposes behind a business. If, for example, Simmons's company is in the red at the end of ten years, the SBA might take into consideration how much the company has helped minorities in the entertainment business and then possibly forgive the debt.

Before considering how New Ventures has functioned, it's worth looking at what the company was first set up to do. New Ventures is a subsidiary of MCA, the conglomerate whose main holding is Universal Studios. Unlike such studios as Warners and Paramount, which are subsidiaries of conglomerates, MCA and Universal are, for most practical purposes, one and the same. The men who make MCA's major decisions are the same men who make Universal's major decisions. Those same men also comprise the board of directors of New Ventures, along with its president and a few others.

This relationship poses problems. It exists because MCA put up the seed money that New Ventures needed in order to get more money from the SBA. The relationship does not stop there. According to Simmons (no longer with New Ventures), he had the right, on behalf of New Ventures, to enter into development deals to buy books or scripts and to hire people to write them. Simmons did not, however, have the power to commit funds unilaterally to the production of a film. To do that—and the SBA allows New Ventures to invest up to $900,000 in a single film—Simmons needed the approval of his board of directors: the leadership of MCA and Universal.

The production power, then, is not in the hands of minorities. It is, instead, in the hands of the people who, as a group or class, have done so little to bring minorities into the film business. The existence of New Ventures is based on the premise that minorities have been unfairly excluded from the entertainment media. The SBA accepts this as a given, and so does Norbert Simmons. By supporting New Ventures, MCA also seems to be saying that it's time to give the minorities a break. A reasonable sentiment, but it raises the issue of hypocrisy. The government seems to be rewarding the very people who have caused the problems, people who could simply have opened their doors a little wider to accommodate more minorities. So why did MCA choose this roundabout way to help minorities?

A possible answer to that question can be found in the structure and financing of New Ventures. MCA executives have full control over how their money will be invested—but it's not just their money. Thanks to SBA leverage, three dollars out of every four invested will have come out of the government's pocket. MCA will use the money to broaden its chances of coming up with a hit. The only stipulation is that the film be made for, about, and/or by minorities. Simmons didn't find cynicism in MCA's motivation for starting New Ventures.

"I think the greatest indication of MCA's motives lies in the fact that we approached them, not the other way around," Simmons says. "I will tell you honestly that we have been a failure as filmmakers, but we've tried. I feel no heat from the leadership of MCA about that.

"There is another issue as well," he continues. "I have had black moviemakers in here, stars, who have had projects made and distributed. They come here because there just is no mechanism to get to the people with the power at the studios. So, I have to say about what we're doing: If not us, who, if not now, when, and if not here, where?" Simmons blames his "failure" as a filmmaker on SBA rules and Hollywood racism. The SBA won't allow the company to put up more than half the financing of a film, and under no circumstance may that amount go over $900,000. Because of these rules Simmons had to seek other sources of financing. He blames racism for his failure to raise additional funds . . . that, and the related problem of finding minority talent with track records. Simmons feels that problem is a symptom of racism, too.

"In Hollywood, you tend to work with those people you play with," he notes. "There just are not a lot of black people living in Beverly Hills. You know, if I had to set up five movie companies using minority people by two days from now, I couldn't do it. If I had to fund ten minority-owned record companies, I could do it by five o'clock today. In the record business there has been the opportunity that does not exist in films. Civil rights once was both ethically correct and chic. Now, it's not chic anymore."

In March of 1980 investments by New Ventures in record companies and legitimate theater productions were keeping the firm running at a profit.

While Simmons criticizes Hollywood, others criticize Simmons. One filmmaker, who approached New Ventures with plans for a multimedia production company, was irritated by New Ventures' refusal of his proposal. "I had a detailed plan for an ongoing small business, and it seems like all they were looking for were specific projects." The purpose of SBICs and MESBICs, our source notes, is to provide the capital for starting small business. Simmons agrees with this concept but says the movie SBICs broadened the definition of a small business to include an entity that wouldn't ordinarily qualify as a business—the entrepreneur/producer. "We had to convince the SBA that the producer was, in a sense, the whole business," recalls Simmons. "And I think that's an accurate way for them to understand the way a producer works. He hires people, pays for services, makes a product. In other words, there is a business cycle there. It's just much shorter than in any other kind of business."

A second criticism voiced by our filmmaker source is that New Ventures has been too conservative in its film investment. Our source feels that more money should be committed by New Ventures to development, but because that tends to be a risky investment, our source asserts New Ventures has shied away from it. Though he acknowledges that development deals that eventually result in profitable films are rare, he cites the SBA's social charter as being a more urgent concern.

The other movie SBICs have had even less success than New Ventures. Originally, six companies were approved by the SBA as part of a three-year pilot program, an act which meant that once they got their seed money, they would be licensed—and the SBA money to make the movies would start to flow. By early 1980 all but one of the companies were inactive. The one active company, International Film Investments (IFI), had at that time invested no government money in any movie. "A lot of the SBICs were put together by the same people who did tax shelters a few years ago," Simmons says. "They thought it was a similar arrangement: I'll put up one dollar and get four. It didn't work out that way. . . . This is a way of maximizing your upside potential; tax shelters maximized the downside."

Stumbling blocks have arisen on both the practical and the philosophical levels. Government red tape, as usual, has slowed the works: After three years of existence the program had not seen any of the SBA's money spent on a film. And in order to qualify for government money, SBICs were expected to raise millions on their own—no easy task for anyone when the investment is going to be as uncertain as film.

There are also questions about the whole idea of the Small Business Administration helping moviemakers. Would this involvement of the government serve to, in effect, underwrite experimental or noncommercial filmmaking? Apparently not. IFI, the only functioning SBIC, has so far used its own money to make *Old Boyfriends* (with Talia Shire and John Belushi) and *Hopscotch* (with Walter Matthau and Glenda Jackson). There's no reason to think that once they have spent the prerequisite $5 million of their own, the forthcoming government money would go off in an entirely different artistic direction, at least not with the SBA emphasis on turning a profit. The *B* stands for business, don't forget.

The *S* stands for small, but so far, the SBICs have failed to encourage low-budget filmmakers or newcomers to the business. Indeed, one of the major criticisms when the film SBICs were announced was that some of the money would go to such entrenched industry types as Telly Savalas and Howard Koch, whose SBIC would later go on to the inactive list.

There is another question too: Should the SBA encourage people to compete toe to toe with other moviemakers for box office dollars? If the SBA gets into film financing in a big way, it will be offering the same goods and services that are now being presented by the studios, mini-majors, and independents, who are privately funded. And who pay taxes.

A reasonably well informed taxpayer may wonder as well why the government would make uncollateralized loans to what has always been a risky business, at least without sharing the profits. The government wondered about it, too, when the SBIC program was set up. But somehow its advisors talked them out of profit sharing. A fair interpretation of the rule is that when a film hits, it will be Malibu and Mercedes for the producer, but when it bombs, that's the taxpayers' problem.

Finally, there is the issue of the government using taxpayer dollars to promote ideologies. The SBA laid down three rules in this area: no X-rated movies, no movies about religion, and no politics. The X-rating rule is the most enforceable, since the rating draws a neat line through the controversy. Films about religion are notorious box office poison, so no one is clamoring to make them. The exact prohibition is against using a film to proselytize for a specific religion, *proselytize* being the key word.

Politics is more subtle. Were *Death Wish* and *Dirty Harry* right-wing propaganda? And what about those youth films of the early 1970s? Politics can be seen in virtually everything from sex to the life-style of the characters on the screen. To narrow this field, according to IFI's Josiah Child, the practical proscription is against films that promote a particular political party. "Under these rules," he adds, "we could have made *All the President's Men.*"

Child's company has found these various restrictions to be less of an obstruction than the raising of funds. Like New Ventures, IFI can't fund more than 50 percent of the budget for any single feature. Finding the rest of the money has been a problem, but a solution was achieved by forming and then affiliating with an English company called Gold Crest. IFI is the largest partner, but the funds of Gold Crest—now at $19 million—will not come from the SBA. The advantage of this arrangement is that the leadership of IFI can commit all the money needed to finance a film.

However, time is running out on the SBIC/MESBIC program. It was announced in 1977 as a "pilot," with a charter of three years. Once that time line is crossed, the government will evaluate the program and decide its future. The betting, though, is that the future will be bleak.

10

DOMESTIC DISTRIBUTION:

"WILL IT PLAY

IN ITABINA?"

THE BASIC GOAL OF FILM DISTRIBUTION IN THIS COUNTRY AND ABROAD is the same one shared by any other business: Get the goods out to the customer. But with movies, complications set in right away. We have seen in the production of pictures that every movie ever made is a prototype, manufactured under conditions that make past experience unnervingly irrelevant, and the way films are distributed inevitably varies from movie to movie as well.

In fact, even the mechanisms used to distribute movies depend on the actual film under consideration—and more importantly, on who is distributing it. Like many of the other central activities of the film business, things look quite a bit different from the vantage point of the studios than from that of the independent. Studios have a setup in place that reflects their stability as business concerns and, because of it, their ability to put a steady stream of movies into the distribution pipeline. Responsibility usually rests with the vice-president of distribution at the studio, who in turn oversees a hierarchy headed by a handful of managers, who each look after an entire region of the country. Below the regional managers on the organization chart come the twenty or so branch managers, assigned to major population centers within each region. Below them are the local managers, who see to the distribution activities of the studio in the big cities or, in less crowded parts of the country, clusters of small towns that together boast enough movie theaters to merit paying the salary of someone to service them.

Independent distributors, on the other hand, have to live with the idea that the producers whose films they handle may not be around tomorrow, as well as the parallel fact of life that, unlike the studios, they cannot guarantee a steady flow of movies to theaters. Generally, whereas the studio system is centralized, with everyone included in distribution paid by the studio, the independent distribution scheme tends to be decentralized. The independent distributor doesn't carry on his activities under a unified corporate umbrella. One film at a time, one deal at a time, the independent distributor places films with a corps of subdistributors in selected territories. Each subdistributor is, in turn, an independent contractor, a partner rather than employee of the distributor. Theoretically, this way of doing things means that everyone is an ally, that they are all small businessmen working to give the film the best break in order also to make money for themselves. More often than not, the loose confederation of equals really means that there is no effective way for anyone to gauge whether or not an effective job of distribution was ever attempted or to improve a sloppy job until it is too late. Independents can't oversee their subdistributors; they can merely suggest persuasively.

There is always a lot of debate in the film business about which distribution setup is the best one. The question seems to be fairly academic. If a producer has a deal with a major studio, that studio will then distribute that film. If you are a producer with a proven track record, or a mini-major with a distribution deal with the studio, you will most likely have something to say about how your film is distributed. On the other hand, if you are a relative newcomer, you will enjoy no more control over the handling of your film than you would if you contracted distribution to an independent distributor. On the other hand, whereas most producers seek out independent distributors only after a studio has turned down their projects, many independent producers feel more comfortable leaving the fate of their films—and their own financial fortunes—to smaller organizations, provided that personal or contractural relationships insure them a voice in how their film gets distributed.

Independent or studio, though, the basic job is the same. Distribution exists to get theater owners to rent movies. The people the distributor may be trying to convince range from the mom-and-pop owners of one or two neighborhood movie houses or drive-ins to the managers of the big theater chains who make the decisions for hundreds of theaters under their control. Distribution, naturally, works very closely with marketing; most independent distributors merge both functions. But where marketing is primarily directed at drawing people into the theaters, distribution is undertaken at a much more personal level, since it tries to convince individual theater owners rather than the public at large to take a chance on a movie.

Many observers theorize that it is in this realm of personal contact and long-time association that the distribution executives at the major studios hold a significant edge over the independents. One of the reasons may be such people as Robert Wilkinson, the man in charge of distributing almost $200 million worth of movies a year for Universal—a company he joined as a local film salesman in 1941.

Wilkinson describes what he does succinctly: "I work with anybody that will work with me, advertising people, the producers, the theater owners, to get maximum revenue out of the product. . . . I do have a national idea; in most of the U.S. I know what I'm doin'. In forty years you'd better learn from your mistakes."

He illustrates what he means, reaching back to the days of the Ma and Pa Kettle films. They were a big hit in urban areas, but in his southern territories, "the chickens runnin' in the fuckin' house and the poverty was too real.

"The appeal of pictures to people is what you have to learn. I tell a lot of these producers: Will it play in Itabina? Itabina's a small town.

You don't have to play there to have a hit, but if they like it in Itabina, you've got a pretty good chance.

"But every picture's different," he sighs. "You can't sell any two of them the same way."

Theater selection is crucial to Wilkinson's work. He says he tries to know most of the theater owners around the country. He also indicates that it is more important to know the theaters. New population centers that spring up, neighborhoods that are changing, movie houses that have just been built, or theaters that are on their last legs are all filed into the memories of such people as Wilkinson. While a movie is still just a script, studio distribution executives sometimes skull out where it should play once it's finished. Those decisions, so crucial to the six-month-to-two-year money-earning lifespan of a film, are usually made on the basis of precedent. In a business in which hunches often carry more weight than demographic research, the box office record of a particular kind of film in a specific theater usually determines the releasing pattern for most future films.

It could be called the rabbit's-foot phenomenon: the idea that if one kind of film does well in one kind of theater, the same kind of film is bound to have at least an equal shot at doing as well.

"Woody Allen films will always play the Regent [in Westwood, the college town just south of UCLA]," says a student of movie bookings who has logged more than a decade of inside observations. "Woody's first theatrical film, *Take the Money and Run,* played there. It established him as a serious filmmaker and made some money. Now he wants all of his films to play that house. It's only four hundred seats, so he'll always fill it up . . . have the line outside the theater. Who wants to go out there and fail?"

If you're misguided enough to attempt a weekend drive through Westwood after dark, it will become glaringly obvious that Woody Allen isn't the only moviemaker who wants to open there. Scorekeepers in London and New York keep a close watch on the weekly take within the precincts of "the Village." Right now, almost any theater in Westwood is considered a hot homestead for a promising film property. A Westwood run carries status, too; producers often feel slighted if a Westwood opening isn't part of the deal they strike with a studio.

Those who seek a rational explanation can point to a set of figures compiled by the Motion Picture Association of America. In a national test sampling of 2,500 people, the MPAA discovered that the major ticket purchasers were between sixteen and twenty years old. Further figures claimed a once-a-month movie attendance for the statistical sample until thirty-nine years of age. In other words, just the type of people who hang out in Westwood—college kids, young execs, and skateboarders, all mingling together in movie lines.

But Westwood is simply not the right place for certain movies to make their first play. "Action pictures, westerns, Clint Eastwood movies will always do better on Hollywood Boulevard," says a Filmways distribution executive. "A good picture in Westwood will always do business on the Boulevard," he continues. "But an action picture won't do well in Westwood. It's a rougher group who go to the Boulevard."

Increasingly, the pattern in Los Angeles is shifting away from "exclusives" (movies at one theater only) to "day and date" (same opening nights on Hollywood Boulevard and in Westwood) or "mini-multiples" (simultaneous openings at eight to ten theaters).

"Everybody in this business follows the same basic breakout," says a distribution executive at Warners. "You're not going to play only Westwood or only the Boulevard. You'll open there, but you'll go to two or three houses in the Valley [San Fernando Valley] and a couple of places in Orange County.

"You've just got to do it that way," he adds. "The geographic spread of the population is a factor, along with relatively easy access to the theaters. When we release a picture, we want to have seats—enough seats so that people will come to see the product."

Even with a collection of locations to choose from, each theater is carefully chosen by its past history and present neighborhood. "We have a duty to evaluate what we think each theater can do. Location is a heavy consideration for us," he says.

"You look at a history of what each theater is capable of doing," echoes an executive who manages the distribution of Disney films for

Buena Vista Productions. "There are houses that get to be known as family houses. The public thinks of them as family oriented. The public is not educated that, say, an adult type of house can play a family film—you follow me? We have to be very careful."

In New York, too, the location for the debut of a film is a crucial consideration. "The way it is in L.A. with Westwood and Hollywood Boulevard is the same with the East Side and Broadway," Wilkinson says. He notes that whereas the legendary "block" on the east side of Third Avenue between Fifty-ninth and Sixtieth streets is still the pinnacle of prestige, Broadway has shed much of its soiled reputation. "Broadway has turned around. I've broken pictures here and had big hits on Broadway with movies I would never have thought of putting there just a while ago. I mean, *Heaven Can Wait* had its single best engagement on Broadway."

As we said earlier, most independent producers rely on independent distributors to take care of choosing theaters and arranging play dates. Often independents find that the major studios have beaten them to the punch—all the desirable times of the year to release a film (Christmas, summertime, other holidays) may be taken up by the studios, along with all the desirable theaters. In those cases, the best an independent can hope for is a five-day engagement anywhere he can find it. If his film draws a crowd, other theaters may decide to rent it, a tortuous process of convincing one theater at a time that you have a hit film on your hands, based on last week's box office figures. One slow week in one slow town, and the film may be finished forever.

Recently, a few of the independent producers have begun to tackle distribution themselves. Edward Montoro, a former private airplane pilot who now heads Film Ventures International (*The Fifth Floor*, *Kill or Be Killed*), explains that his staff is made up of people who used to work at American International Pictures before that company was swallowed up by Filmways. Film Ventures International employs a sales manager, branch managers, accountants, and specialists who monitor the number and location of prints of current FVI releases. Carrying the similarity to the studios further, Montoro reports, "We use subdistributors very, very rarely; when we do, it is people we have a franchise agreement with, so we know what they're doing all of the time." Montoro enters into negotiations directly with all of the major theater chains, apparently not feeling comfortable entrusting that crucial chore to anyone else. "The chains make or break a company like ours. They may have 850 screens apiece, and you have to talk to only one guy to get on all of those 850 screens. It's just what the majors do.

"From time to time," he continues, "we have thought of going to the other indies and suggesting we all get together to set up a distribution company for all of us. But the really independent production companies are run by people with a really independent streak. The question comes up of who will be the boss of the distribution company. Then it all kind of falls apart, since none of us is in this to be bossed by anyone else."

Montoro also makes it clear that he isn't envious of the studios.

"It's just a different ball game. I could not have handled, say, a James Bond movie as well as United Artists could. I don't have the resources. But by the same token, I have to be as aggressive in what we do as the majors. We can't sit back and complain."

Not surprisingly, Montoro has also endeavored to match the studios' edge in a very difficult area—regularly released product.

"We were, and in many ways we still are, a marketing company. We pick up films other people have produced and market them. But we have turned to production for one reason: We feel we need to control the kind and quality of at least half of the films we put out. We can't just release what happens to stagger through the door." One of Montoro's maxims is, "I don't care what a film cost to make. That has nothing to do with its value. The only value a film has is what you can get out of it." In order to beef up his catalogue with more films that have the value he is looking for, Montoro himself reads every script and makes the decisions about whether to produce a project or pass it up. He also designs the marketing and distribution strategies for the films his company releases.

"A lot of the films that we buy are already made. I feel that we can use them as filler for a drive-in or a theater that still plays a double feature. You make the deal on the movie you think will be a winner; you let the guy rent the filler for a flat two hundred bucks and you just forget it."

Another important area of distribution to independents and studios alike is the sale of films to television. Here, too, there is what might be called a difference in approach. A studio production, unless it's a smash, will garner a television sale of less than a million dollars, much less if the film is sold as part of a package that includes three or four other movies. Now, the studios, like everybody else, can always use a million dollars. But that money is often simply used to improve the profit picture of a losing film. Even in the case of a hit, much the same situation applies: Although television sales figures may reach into multiples of a million dollars, that revenue serves as an additional profit for a film that is already successful. TV sales (both to pay and commercial TV) are also a form of insurance, in that they help guarantee that a film will at least break even.

Television sales are vital to the survival of independents. Montoro states flatly, "We have to have that TV sale." But reflecting his bottom-line–based view of his business, he also points out, "You've got to hit that box office really well. You can have a $2 million sale to a network lined up, and it will go out the window if nobody comes to the film."

Sometimes, people come to the theater—a lot of them—and, somehow, after all of the money has been collected, the picture doesn't seem to have made a profit. Or not a big enough profit to share with anyone other than the independent distributor or the studio distribution organization. Producer, director, stars are all out of luck. This leads to the most serious charge leveled against distributors, regardless of size or stature: outright theft.

As in most sorts of white collar crime, the alleged robbery is almost always accomplished through accounting. Producers, stars, and directors who work for a fee plus a percentage or either gross revenue or profits continually claim they have been stiffed on a hit film by the distributor. Usually, the charge is that the distributor has padded the expenses for the trinity of things distributors are called on to pay for: prints, promotion, and advertising.

"Anytime the picture started to show a profit, they said, 'Oops, here's another bill for prints.' Or ads, or something. I never saw a penny," complains one producer. Although independent sales organizations as well as the majors come in for about equal shares of accusations, little is ever done. Novice producers usually settle out of court, if at all, with independent distributors; well-known names do the same at the studios. When Sean Connery and Michael Caine sued Allied Artists (the company filed for bankruptcy in 1980) over the accounting of profits for *The Man Who Would Be King,* it created a furor in the industry. Not at the allegation itself, but at the fact that the two stars had "gone public" about a crime that is almost an accepted business practice.

"I looked at the books and we were getting checks, all right, but the checks just weren't big enough for the kind of business the movie was doing," one producer told us about another studio. "She [the star] and I had a percentage of the gross, and it looked like they were paying us a percentage of the net; in other words, of every dollar *after their expenses* instead of every dollar. I figured: an innocent mistake. So I called up to tell them what happened. They told me it wasn't a mistake, they were paying net. One guy said if I didn't like it, I should sue. We finally settled out of court, for fifty cents on the dollar of what they really owed us."

But there are other accounting practices that cause an outcry. The principal bone of contention seems to be the mixing together of two methods of accounting, cash and accrual. The cash method calls for accounts to be credited at the time when money is collected and debited at the time when it is spent. Accrual methods of accounting call for logging credits and debits not when they actually occur, but when they are put on the books. In most businesses—and on your income tax return—one *or* the other technique is used. The film business, at least at the studios, employs both accounting methods simultaneously as standard practice; many charge that the studios switch from one method to the other whenever it does them the most good and the profit participants the most harm. (In an article cataloguing a series of charges against 20th Century-Fox by the producers of *Alien*, the Los Angeles *Times* pointed out that Fox debited the accounts of the film when it committed money it had not yet spent but failed to credit its accounts until income had actually been collected.)

But distributors themselves are also plagued with theft. Theater owners deflate the nightly take for the reports they are required to file with the distributors, and keep the difference. Or they don't tear tickets but sell the same batch again, reporting only the second sale —a con employees can run without the knowledge of the theater owner. "We spend a lot of time and money on policing, just so people know they are being policed," notes Universal's Wilkinson. "It's very expensive—oh, yes—and very necessary to remove temptation.

"Say you own a theater back in Mississippi and you live out here in L.A. Maybe you got a young cashier, and maybe she's got a sick child at home, real sick, and she doesn't have much money. She's handling ten thousand a week for you. She doesn't consider it stealing; she means to pay it back. Of course," he adds, his voice turning a bit menacing, "there are people who are just thieves. I can spot that stuff a mile away by this time."

He drags another story out of his attic of experiences with theater owners. "I called up one of my very best friends in this business—he's recently passed away—and said, 'Goddamnit, are you stealing—from *me*?' You know what he said? 'I sure as hell am. My wife is dying of cancer and if I can't steal from you, I'll rob a bank.' " Wilkinson claims the man later made full restitution.

The standard way for both distributors and theater owners to guard against theft is to employ "checkers." Theater owners pay people to count the number of people in the theater and compare their count with the number of tickets sold. Distributors hire people to make sure that the theater owners are giving them as honest a count as possible. Checkers are always unknown to the people they are checking up on; they appear at any time. The threat of surprise is meant to carry its own warning. For, as Bob Wilkinson philosophises, "The first guy who gets his hands on your money has you at a disadvantage."

FOREIGN DISTRIBUTION:

"WE BRING A WORTHLESS
PIECE OF FILM IN, AND WE
BRING DOLLARS OUT"

IT'S HAPPENED TO JUST ABOUT EVERYBODY WHO HAS SPENT EVEN A couple of days in a foreign country. You're walking along, taking in the sights and sounds of unfamiliar experiences, when all of a sudden a poster advertising an American movie splashes across the wall of a kiosk. Sometimes the names of the stars or the distinctive logo of the film are recognizable. More often, a lucky guess tells you that the advertisement you're puzzling over bears some resemblance to a film you've seen back home. On other occasions, you may never have heard of the movie at all; you're left wondering what in the world a favorite actor is doing in a foreign film.

American movie posters are a common sight in other countries because movies made in America are one of the most popular cargoes in world trade today. In Sweden, the former home of Ingmar Bergman, 60 to 70 percent of all the tickets sold are for American films. Americans may flock to the fluffy comedies of the French, or ponder the mysteries of such German directors as Herzog or Fassbinder, but in Germany and France, Walt Disney's *The Rescuers* is among the top-grossing films of all time.

Like all foreign trade, it's a two-way street. As much as foreigners seem to have an unabated appetite for movies stamped "made in America," producers and distributors in this country depend on revenue generated abroad. Recent estimates place the major studios' share of the profit pie contributed by foreign sales as high as 40 percent of total revenue. More often than not, independents depend upon selling overseas distribution rights to their films in advance, as a way to secure production capital. On whatever end of the industry spectrum people do business, it is clear that foreign sales are important.

Foreign distribution is taken care of under one of two mutually exclusive sets of arrangements. Basically, the studios accomplish foreign distribution one way; everyone else does it another. Studios operate overseas pretty much the same way they do at home. The studios maintain their own offices and staffs in foreign markets, and, in so doing, they control their own distribution machinery. Under the studio system of foreign distribution, accounting is also centralized. Profits and losses from the total overseas take of each film are thrown together; profits from one country or market territory make up—hopefully—for losses in another.

Independents and mini-majors do things a great deal differently. They depend on a series of deals made with independent distributors on a country-by-country or territory-by-territory basis. In their simplest form, the deal struck involves the payment of a negotiated cash guarantee by the distributor to the independent or mini-major in exchange for the exclusive right to sell a film in a specified foreign market.

An executive at Lorimar explains a typical foreign distribution deal involving mini-majors or independents like this: "We'll call the country 'x' and this will be a typically structured distribution deal. The distributor in country 'x' gives the producer (Lorimar, for example) a guarantee of, let's say, $100,000."

In the case we're sketching here, the payment of $100,000 secures for the distributor the exclusive right to show the film in territories or theaters under his control. As we have just noted, the guarantee is negotiated. Guarantee haggling is based on the number of theater seats under the sway of the distributor, past performance of similar films with similar audiences, and an estimate of the point at which the foreign client will be alienated from the process by a foolishly high guarantee demand from the production company. Guarantees also have a snowballing value, an effect that is easy enough to visualize when the hypothetical $100,000 figure is multiplied by several countries or territories.

On the production side of the deal, producers are assumed to sleep a little more soundly, comforted by the knowledge of guaranteed cash in the safe even if their films are dreadful failures at the theaters. Often, this money is used to help finance the film at hand.

To return to our executive:

"When the distributor starts to get his money back from the theaters, he gets to keep the first $200,000. The first $100,000 of that amount pays him back for the guarantee money he laid out. The next $50,000 pays him back for the costs of prints of the film and advertising. The next $50,000 after that, he keeps as his profit. Whatever else comes in after this first $200,000 is then split on a fifty-fifty basis with the producer."

In this highly speculative corner of the movie business, foreign film distributors who work with mini-majors and independents need ready cash and good instincts. Some foreign distributors put hundreds of thousands of dollars on the line based on a peek at the cast list of a film or a hearty word about its chances from the producer.

Edward Sarlui, a Latin American distributor, looks at what he does this way: "We bring in an essentially worthless piece of film and we bring dollars out. Nobody knows what value to place on an unreleased film. It's a feeling."

Some foreign film buyers are trying to take some of the mystery out of the transaction, but most are resigned to their fate. "I'm trapped in Tokyo," says Sam Namba, one of the largest distributors of American movies to Japan. "They send the scripts, I read them. I give them a letter of credit and they use it to make a movie. It's rare that the picture I see a year later is the picture I envisioned in the script."

One of the more intriguing factors that make up one of the costs for distributors overseas lies in the oft-forgotten fact that not everyone everywhere speaks English. Or even American. So subtitles are a problem, not only in rendering American slang into Japanese ideograms, but also across smaller distances: Scandinavian distributors groan at the fiscally important fact that there are over 250 more words in the Danish language than in the Swedish language.

More important, distributors often find their entrepreneurial instincts curbed by censorship.

Walter E. Senior is a casually well-dressed man in his early forties who distributes American films to all South American countries but Mexico and Argentina. "Argentina has the worst censorship of any South American country towards any suggestion of sex or violence," Senior asserts. "In Brazil they are very concerned with anything that seems to be against the law, or against authority. *Convoy* was banned because what the trucks in the movie were doing was illegal."

Producers, particularly independents and mini-majors, have their problems, too, centering around the acquisition of superstar talent.

Usually, deals with the biggest box office stars are negotiated for a fee plus a percentage of the gross box office revenue generated by their films. Although most of the mini-majors and even a few independents are often willing and able to match the fees demanded by the superstars, they have until recently lost out to the studios in the talent-bidding wars. The studios have generally been able to snare the stars through their practice of centralized accounting. With profits and losses from all overseas activity in one pot, marquee-name stars can easily monitor the amounts owed to them from first dollar to last.

But the independents and mini-majors, working out their arrangements country by country, have a much more complicated accounting problem on their hands. Returning to the model we cited a moment ago, the mini-major or independent won't get any money until after $200,000 has been taken in at the box office. But the star is still owed his percentage—from the first dollar that came in until the last. That percentage has to come out of the pocket of the mini-major or independent—or else out of the guarantee. Minis and indies have been loath to let either happen.

Even though the studios have tended to win the bankable talent in the past, thanks to their centralized methods of accounting, they are beginning to lose ground. The major reason lies with a practice called cross-collateralization.

"Let's say it costs a studio $300,000 to open a picture in France," hypothesizes one distribution executive for Avco-Embassy. "That's for prints and advertising. Let's say the picture doesn't do anything there. That's a $300,000 loss, right? Well, with the studios, that's going to wipe out the profits from a lot of other countries, isn't it?"

"Every picture has a weak territory," says Lorimar president Merv Adelson axiomatically. "Few films will appeal in every area internationally."

Mini-majors and the more active independents are hoping that they can convince the stars—and their agents—that compartmentalized deals on a country-by-country basis actually mean a better deal for the "gross players." They reason that the big-name stars will be attracted by the fact that the profits reaped by films in one country will not be jeopardized should the film flop somewhere else in the world. This policy has apparently begun to pay off.

The foreign distribution scene is further complicated by the question of who holds the power—or who needs whom the most. One foreign distributor observes, "It's always a seller's market; we are dependent upon product, upon having something to show. That's how we make our money." But Walter Senior disagrees. "It's both a buyer's and seller's market, usually," he says, adding wryly, "but it switches from a buyer's to a seller's depending on the film." These questions of relative clout don't apply to the studios, since the distinction between buyer and seller evaporates because of studio ownership of foreign distribution of their movies.

If the partnership between independent producers and independent distributors tends to change from film to film, there is still one area where production ardently craves what distribution has to offer: cash.

The guarantee paid by distributors is always paid "in front," that is, in advance of the exhibition of the movie. Most of the time, though, the guarantee is collected not only before the film is shown but before it is even completed. In that case, all of the sales to all of the foreign distributors make up *completion money,* money that is needed to finish the film.

As we have seen, foreign sales are important to the mini-majors as a source of production capital; they are even more critical to the independents and their investors. At the other end of the spectrum projects under consideration at studios must pack a foreign appeal, often indicated by an estimate projecting country-by-country ticket sales, in order to secure approval.

"It's a difficult dialogue when you talk about completion," says Senior. "They want to control creative decisions, yet, for our part, we're putting up the money and voting not only for the picture we buy but also for similar types of pictures."

Another distributor shrugs off his partner's discomfort. "I want to get films at the lowest price. I can get them at a low price by putting up my guarantee, by putting up my money, before anyone else does."

Getting a better price on a potential hit is also a source of indirect profits for the independent foreign distributors. In many countries large distributors are both buyers and sellers, purchasing film rights for an entire territory and selling off chunks of it. But the guarantee is doing something else, too. It is providing the kind of insurance domestic moviemaking has never known—profit insurance. Imagine you are gambling $2 million or more to make an epic version of your summer at Yellowstone. If you can convince Walter Senior in South America to buy the distribution rights to your film for $1.5 million, if a distributor in Sweden does the same for $1 million, and Sam Namba wants in for $3 million, consider what you have wrought: You have made your film, and you have made a huge profit. Not only that, but every dime you take in from domestic ticket sales, television rights, or T-shirts is additional profit.

This wish for safety in an unsafe trade has confronted us lately with what is being called the international film. At its crudest, the international film is a collection of stars and a synthesis of stories that promise worldwide commercial appeal. If, for example, most of Western Europe, Japan, and South America goes crazy for action and science fiction, the ideal international film will blend both components into a story. If these countries like the same gross players as we do in the United States, those players will all be in the international film—along with names lesser known in the States but capable of packing people in throughout Latin America. The international film is the closest thing the movie business has to a product that is designed by market research focused on what people have bought in the past. *A Bridge Too Far,* which welded a war story to cameo appearances by a long roster of gross players, is one example of the international film. So, too, are most of the *Airport* movies and Irwin Allen's disaster cartoons.

Even though income from foreign distribution is vitally important to moviemaking in the United States, foreign movies rarely succeed in the United States, and the international films seem to do lukewarm business among American audiences, too. Recently, the head of the government-financed agency to promote British film production proclaimed that the industry in his country "effectively no longer existed, with U.S. movies accounting for 75 percent of the U.K. box office." In China, with a thousand theaters, leaders are looking for American movies—and it seems pretty clear no trade paper headline is likely soon to read "PEKING PIC BOFFO ON U.S. SCREENS."

So, at a time when Americans are depressed by evidence that the prestige and power of their country is waning, it might be argued that our influence has never been greater. At least down at the local movie house.

12

BLIND BIDDING:
THE BATTLE AT
THE MOVIE HOUSE

GOING TO A MOVIE IS AN EXPERIENCE WITH WHICH MOST OF US ARE quite familiar. You pay your money, get a ticket, and anchor the soles of your shoes to a gooey miasma of day-old soft drinks spilled on the floor, while the film unwinds up there on the screen. On the surface it all seems rather straightforward. But for the past several years the local movie house, drive-in, or multiplex has become a battleground between two of the groups who together have traditionally gained the most from hits and suffered the most from flops: the distributors, who get the movies into the theaters, and the exhibitors, or theater owners. The fierceness of the fight, some observers say, could spell the beginning of the end for the movie business.

The skirmishing is all the more striking because distributors and exhibitors—despite occasional squabbles—used to get along so well. In fact, at one time the major studios acted as *both* exhibitor and distributor. They owned the talent, made the movies—one a week, to feed the movie habit of a growing nation—and delivered them to the theaters. Conveniently enough, the studios owned most of the theaters, too, accounting for the telltale "Fox" or "Warner" still lurking in disconnected neon above the marquees of many big-city movie palaces.

Production, distribution, exhibition. All the commercial functions of the movie business linked together trunk to tail, like elephants in a circus parade, all controlled by the studios. The advantages of such a setup for the studios were enormous. Scheduling, advertising, the success of a hit or the fizzle of a flop were all reported instantly, so that profits could be boosted and losses cut. As an added bonus, there was nobody in the middle to take a slice of the profit.

But the United States Justice Department, long a sorehead about what they perceive as closed commercial systems, rained on the parade. Starting in July 1938, they sued Paramount Pictures and the other studios, charging them with monopolistic practices. Studio lawyers responded; the crawl through the courts was on. There was a break for World War II, and then in 1946 the new class of independent theater owners put pressure on the Justice Department, charging that the studios were booking their best films into their own theaters while feeding the leavings to the independents. The independent owners complained that they were not allowed to offer terms to secure the good material for their screens in a climate of competitive bidding. It seemed to government lawyers that the potential for the restraint of trade they had claimed in the late 1930s had been realized in the late 1940s.

In addition to the tendency toward a stranglehold on production, distribution and exhibition—lawyers call this vertical ownership—another thing bothered the government. Federal probers were also worked up about the horizontal ownership of large numbers of studio-controlled theaters as a threat to individual entrepreneurship.

A whole bundle of claims and counterclaims finally reached the Supreme Court during the late 1940s and the early 1950s. The Court found that the five companies among the eight major studios having a significant involvement in theater ownership were indeed operating in a way that indicated monopolistic practices and the restraint of trade. The Court gave the studios the unhappy choice of deciding which area of activity to jettison. The moguls decided to get rid of exhibition and keep distribution and production. The findings by the

Court are known euphemistically in the industry as consent decrees, since the studios essentially pleaded no contest to a set of decisions they would have been required to accept eventually anyhow. Industry lawyers further sweetened the lexicon by calling the Supreme Court decisions "the Paramount decrees," after the luckless studio that was the first to be sued.

Those consent decrees handed down three decades ago are very much on industry minds right now.

It isn't that the basic issues are any longer in doubt. Studios rather quietly gave up the screens they held. Since then, huge chains of theaters have sprung up, owned by individuals or national corporations with hundreds of screens apiece. Ironically, such companies as Loew, Mann, or Plitt have occasionally been called on the judicial carpet for the same horizontal ownership of screens that was once the problem with the studios.

Besides the national movie chain owners, there are lots of regional giants, too—for example, Northeast Theater Corporation or, in the West, Metropolitan Theaters. Some theater chains have produced films or invested in new production. Ted Mann of Mann Theaters took a fling. General Cinema, owner of more screens in the country than anyone else, financed a clutch of unpopular pictures before abandoning production. In 1975 an Oregon theater circuit owner came up with the idea for an Exhibitor's Production and Distributor's Cooperative (EX-PRODICO). The notion was that exhibitors across the country would pool their money to make movies. It looked like a good idea: Theater owners would no longer be exclusively dependent on other people for what they could show. City National Bank put up $3 million, provided the exhibitors would match the amount. The Oregon theater owner invested $250,000 of his own money. But in January 1979 it was announced that EXPRODICO had died an embarrassing death. Exhibitors had failed to collectively cough up the needed matching money to get the enterprise off the ground.

The chains, and the remaining owners of only one or two movie houses, are represented by two powerful trade groups, the National Association of Theater Owners (or NATO) and National Independent

Theatre Exhibitors (NITE), respectively. Both groups have developed a hearty dislike for the group that represents the studios, the Motion Picture Association of America (MPAA), headed by former confidant and friend of Lyndon Johnson, Jack Valenti.

Despite these antagonisms, theater owners and the MPAA have agreed in the past to disagree: Their mutual survival depends on a smooth working relationship. If the movies being made cannot be shown, the entire business would have to fold. And that is exactly what pessimistic observers are worried about. The conflict is being waged over the very tie that binds the combatants together: economics.

The picture palaces you go to on Saturday nights pay the distributors for the movies you have paid cash to see. This payment is called a rental. There is an old saw in the movie business to the effect that theaters make all of their real money from popcorn and overpriced candy, but nobody would ever eat the stuff if there weren't a film to go along with it . . . and the more popular the film, the more people to buy that popcorn.

So each movie house manager, rightly enough, wants to show the hit pictures and shun the bombs. Since theater overhead, called the *house nut*, is the same every day whether the gallery is gaping or stuffed, theater staffs, like the distributors, depend on hits making up for flops and know that too many flops means one is out of business.

All of which means that studios like to have hits, too. Once blessed with a film they think is going be successful, they try to maximize box office return. Studio salespeople look at two kinds of income in order to get the most out of the box office. The first is short-term income, the amount of money a theater guarantees for the right to screen a given film. Secondly, and of potentially greater importance, is the total take, revenue collected at the box office over the run of the film. The specific amounts depend in large part on the studios finding the right theaters for the right films, choices that naturally differ with each film.

The studios determine the best mesh of all this by asking for bids from each theater in an area for each film they plan to release. By law the bids are competitive; the theater that comes up with the largest nonreturnable cash guarantee gets the picture in question for a set number of weeks. Since the theaters, too, want to show the kind of movie that appeals to the people who usually patronize their theater, this match is successful in most cases. (That is, rural theaters don't show Ingmar Bergman movies, and downtown theaters will usually show broad comedies and action films.)

The bidding system was working fairly well for a fairly long time. In fact, until recently it seemed to be working better than ever. During the two decades following the consent decrees a whopping 800 lawsuits were filed by exhibitors who went to court squawking that a competitor had entered into a conspiracy with a studio to deprive them of salable films, but during the past decade the rate dropped to ten or twelve actions a year.

Today that understanding and the system that holds it together are breaking apart, and a lot of industry people are worried about the extent of the wreckage. The MPAA and the exhibitor groups are openly hostile toward each other, and the future looks bleak.

It's all happening over a practice called blind bidding, in which studios call upon theater owners to bid competitively for a film they have yet to see.* Typically, about six months before a film's scheduled date of release, the studio sends a "bid letter" to exhibitors. The bid letter describes the film, highlighting the all-star cast, the gifted director, the dynamite screenplay, and the surefire appeal of the project.

The bid letter asks as well as tells. It asks the theater owner to meet or beat a nonreturnable cash-guarantee figure as a condition for getting the film. The bid letter stipulates a minimum playing time for the film, sometimes as much as twelve weeks, and a suggested cut of the take, often 90 percent to the studio and 10 percent to the theater. Theater owners get their overhead off the top, before the split is made, but the overhead sum must also be negotiated in advance.

---

*Since the budgets of independent producers and distributors will usually not allow for the expense of a big star on the marquee, the indies are forced to screen their films for theater owners before securing a bid. Hence, they are immune from the current blind-bidding wrangle, since blind bidding is a "luxury" they have never enjoyed. However, the mini-majors, since their films are distributed by the major studios, are very much involved in this controversy.

The studios, represented by the MPAA, say blind bidding is a necessary evil of the current state of the business. Often, say MPAA staff attorneys, there is a breathtakingly short interval between the time a film is completed and its scheduled release date. (MPAA attorney Judy Freiss says it was a week between the completion and release of *Star Wars*.) A multimillion-dollar film languishing in a can while screenings for theater owners took place and bookings were set up could cost the studio millions just in interest. As an example, some who side with the MPAA say that on a $25 million picture such as *Superman*, a wait would mean a loss of around $2 million a year, or hundreds of thousands of dollars a month, in interest.

The theater owners counter with the argument that a forced commitment to a film they haven't seen robs them of the opportunity to make a truly informed business decision. Sumner Redstone, president of Northeast Theater Corporation, has charged that blind bidding is a form of price fixing. Theater owners, he says, have to accept the studio's terms, without a chance to judge the relative merits of the film they are bidding on.

One argument privately used by the studios to counter complaints about blind bidding goes something like this: The picture business is risky, which everybody knows. We, the studios, take a big risk in backing any movie since *we* get no guarantee of profits when we commit millions. Why should we take all of the risk and you, the theater owners, simply come in at the last and share the profit? Since you're not willing to gamble with us, we find your demands insupportable.

Even more bluntly—and even more privately—studio distribution executives also offer the claim that doing away with blind bidding will not magically insure the theater owners against making their own mistakes. Most of them are eager to tell one or two stories about films that were screened ahead of time for theater owners, backed by their large cash guarantees, and later turned out to be disastrous at their box offices.

The theater owners counter with their own point of view: The payment of a nonreturnable cash guarantee by us in effect takes the gamble out of the deal for you, the distributors. If you can get enough money pledged from us for a shaky film ahead of its release—a film you may have seen and we have not—then you make money even if word of mouth condemns the picture to the doldrums where it belongs. You don't get killed in that eventuality, we do. Especially if we have pledged to show the turkey for a previously arranged number of weeks. Not only that, continue the theater owners, but the 90–10 percent split specified in most bid letters doesn't exactly mean we share fully in the profits, even if our hunch on a film we haven't seen results in a hit in the theater.

And so on. No matter which side commands your allegiance, it's clear that the battle will rage on for some time to come. It's a battle that is recording some pretty nasty skirmishes of late.

Currently, nineteen states and Puerto Rico, or 40 percent of the total national box office, have laws on the books declaring blind bidding to be illegal.* During the early spring of 1978 the MPAA, alarmed at the trend, began to fight back. Valenti, a master politician, went to work lobbying, cajoling, and campaigning. When these techniques of persuasion failed, he sued.

In February 1979 Valenti met with Marvin Goldman, a past president of NATO described by the trade papers as "the chief architect of the offensive on blind bidding." Valenti had come to negotiate. Sitting in on the session were the head of United Artists Theater Circuit and the top man at Loew's theater chain. Releasing an optimistic joint statement on March 5, Valenti's group announced that prospects were good that an industrywide accord on the blind-bidding controversy would be ready for presentation to the NATO board of directors at their annual meeting later that month. Sources who were in on the talks reported that the agreement prescribed a ratio of the number of films a studio would be able to blind-bid each year to the total number of films released during that year. The bigger the output,

*These states, in the order they passed blind-bidding bans, are Louisiana, Virginia, Alabama, South Carolina, Ohio, Utah, Georgia, Idaho, West Virginia, New Mexico, Tennessee, Washington, North Carolina, Maine, Oregon, Massachusetts, Indiana, Pennsylvania, and Kentucky.

the greater number of blind-bid films to be permitted. Valenti was characterized as comfortable with the agreement, and his studio clients seemed happy, too—despite the fact that the real giants among them could supposedly release a handful of junky movies as filler in order to increase the number of occasions on which they would be able to blind-bid a potential blockbuster. NATO also seemed satisfied, even though it wanted a clause placing an absolute ceiling on the total of blind-bid films per releasing season.

But the Justice Department looked askance at a powwow between exhibition and distribution, citing possible antitrust implications. Taking a week to think about it, Justice announced it could brook no agreement. Later, its position was amended to the ambiguous utterance that it would take the question of further contacts between exhibition and distribution "under advisement."

While Valenti was jawboning, the lawyers he pays were in court, challenging the Ohio ban on blind bidding as unconstitutional in that it interfered with interstate commerce, a province of law left to the federal government, not to the states. Since Ohio was the largest state in terms of total box office revenue to approve the ban on blind bidding, the MPAA clearly hoped that a ruling for it in that state would jeopardize current blind-bidding statutes in the other no-blind-bid states. More than a year later, in July 1980, a federal judge supported the NATO position and let the ban on blind bidding stand. Prior to the Ohio court contest, Valenti had returned to an arena and a state he knows intimately: Texas, the third largest state in paid box office admissions (after California and New York). In May 1979 Valenti emerged victorious from a campaign to beat the initiative against blind bidding at the polls.

These slow, costly, and in some cases equivocal methods were starting to make some of the big studios impatient. Studio heads are used to getting what they want by pushing a button—so they began to do just that. Major studios announced a boycott of all new film product to New Mexico, a celluloid blockade that cracked when United Artists offered *Apocalypse Now* for public bid following scheduled prescreenings. North Carolina was also blacked out, preceding all the other states that voted for the end of blind bidding.

Currently, studios have backed off a bit, instituting a practice of negotiating directly with the theaters they have elected to do business with in each state. NATO general counsel Peter Fishbein doesn't like it much, asserting that this negotiation arrangement with theaters sidesteps open public bidding and stifles true competition. The studios contend that they are doing their best with a bad situation, explaining that the open-bid process can take ten days to two weeks, whereas a deal negotiated over the phone takes a matter of hours. Some exhibitors say they are uneasy about the trend toward negotiating. They insist there is a message hidden in the practice: No blind bidding means no chance to bid at all. The Justice Department is apparently looking into the practice but has yet to issue an unequivocal statement concerning this practice, called tracking.

For its part, distribution maintains it often needs to get tough because of unfair, inconvenient clauses in the collection of differently worded anti-blind-bidding statutes in the nineteen states that have outlawed the practice. In some states the studios have gone along with screening their product, albeit grudgingly. But they have tended to cut off new film releases to other states altogether. Prime boycott candidates have been states that account for a relatively modest share of the national total box office but that have tougher laws banning nonreturnable cash guarantees or stipulating that films must be screened for bids in every large city.

By far the most outwardly threatening stance taken by any studio was adopted by Warners. Jay Emmet, of the office of the president of parent Warner Communications (WCI), told a group of leading New Yorkers—including Governor Hugh Carey—that if the defeat of blind bidding cleared the polls in that state, studio interest in shooting films in New York "would be severely reduced." With an estimated $1 billion coming to New York from one hundred projects set to film there this year, a boycott by one of the majors carries a lot of weight. Privately, rumors circulated that WCI had also sent word that if laws against blind bidding were to pass in the Empire State, the corporation would take its corporate headquarters elsewhere. Emmet's announcement in the second largest box office state in the land came at a time when New York officials were kicking off a drive to attract more moviemakers as a source of revenue and jobs. Predictably, Governor Carey has gone on record against blind-bidding bans.

Observers have also noticed lately that studios have stretched the time between bidding and the scheduled release date of some films. Studio sources say confidentially that asking in April for bids on a film scheduled to be released about the time Santa slides down the chimney lets them secure their offers and set their theaters before any more states approve a shutdown of blind bidding. This version is, of course, publicly denied; the studios claim that stiffer competition for the right theaters has made the longer time lag necessary.

This practice has gotten the studios into some trouble lately. In early 1980 United Artists released a movie made by Lorimar called *Cruising*. Concerned with a detective on the trail of a homicidal maniac who murders homosexuals, the picture earned an "R" rating from the MPAA Code and Ratings Board. Giant General Cinema bid on the film blind, entering into an exhibition contract with United Artists. Once the executives of General Cinema got a look at what they had bid on, all bets were off—and the lawsuits were on. General Cinema claimed it has a policy of not showing those movies that, in their judgment, should be tagged "X," so they pulled *Cruising* out of twenty-six theaters. UA sees that move as a simple breach of contract.

The case is worth going into, regardless of its specific outcome, because one of the most recently lodged complaints against blind bidding by theater owners is that the "sensibilities" of patrons cannot be protected by a theater owner who has been forced to bid on a film before it has been screened. Observers say that this argument could go a long way toward swaying legislators in states with anti-blind-bidding bills under consideration.

Finally, perhaps the most telling indication of the sorry state of relations between theater owners and MPAA came in September 1979. In an industry attuned to symbols and what they seem to auger, Jack Valenti was not invited to speak before the annual NATO convention, the first snub in his thirteen-year term of office. He was back in 1980, in a conciliatory mood. But in 1979 he released the following statement: "As I predicted at last year's convention, the blind-bidding issue has turned into a war . . . causing more venom and more blood to be spilled than any other issue in the history of the industry."

A. Alan Friedberg, then president of NATO and a leading Boston exhibitor who spearheaded the defeat of blind bidding in his state, explained why Valenti was not invited: "Exhibition pretty much knows what [he] will say."

Actually, neither side is likely to say anything new, regardless of the year. The defeat or adoption of anti-blind-bid legislation by a particular state, or the ruling on a single case in a single court, will be claimed by one side or the other as a victory. But it is clear that some sort of negotiation offers the only potential for a settlement that will last.

Barry Reardon, a man who was a senior vice-president for General Cinema and is now vice-president and general sales manager for Warners, has been on both sides of the split between exhibition and distribution. He told us simply: "We need each other. I hope we can get this thing settled in the best interest of both groups, so we can get back to making money."

13

MARKETING

WITH EVER-INCREASING BUDGETS AT RISK, THERE IS A GROWING AWARE-
ness of the importance of marketing in the movie business—an importance that nearly every other business has acknowledged for decades.
The volume of output from the studios is staggering, in relation to the
output of a packaged goods company. A satisfied customer might
return again and again for a refill of his favorite cleanser, but new
experience is what the movies must sell. Each studio can reasonably
be seen as a manufacturing company that puts out twenty to thirty new
products a year, each with a terrifyingly short "shelf life." That is,
movies are perishable.

Marketing, for films, has two definitions. One is giving the public
what they want; the other is making the public want what you've got.
In the eyes of many movie marketers, this amounts to a very clear
distinction between "bad" and "good." The principle they see is easily
understood: In other industries, it's common sense to give the public
what they want—small cars that use less gas, permanent-press clothing,
fast food. But in an industry that at least has the pretense of selling
that special commodity, creativity, it has to be the artists who lead the

public, not the other way around. If all the movies ever did was give the public sequels, remakes, and copies, the medium would become, in the words of one marketer, "television. That's where they do that, always giving the public what they want." In other words, the public leads the creators, not the other way around.

As it stands today in the film business, there is a blend of both definitions of marketing—often an unknowing and unarticulated blend. The same studio that is willing to take a chance on financing a small, quirky film might also be in the midst of producing a sequel to an earlier blockbuster.

The problem is that there's usually no sure way to tell what the public wants. Producers can watch the trade paper reports of grosses, but the numbers for one film can never predict how the next one will do. In the mid 1970s, there were three kinds of films one did not make: science fiction, sports, and Vietnam. The films in those subject categories had all bombed, so it was assumed the public was turned off by the subject matter. Vietnam was depressing, science fiction was only for buffs, and who wanted to see movies about boxing or football when they could see real sports events at home, live and for free? In their execution, *Star Wars, Coming Home,* and *Rocky* (as well as *The Deer Hunter* and *Apocalypse Now*) buried those arguments forever, but the same thinking persists. For example, the presence of stars in the cast is said to be insurance that a film will be successful, but in both *Star Wars* and *Rocky,* there were no marquee names. Meanwhile, *Lucky Lady,* with stars Burt Reynolds, Liza Minnelli, and Gene Hackman, proved that some kinds of insurance don't mean very much.

There has to be some method of predicting audience acceptance, and filmmakers hope that marketing research might be it. When the studios first started making use of research and statistics, they employed outside companies, experts in the field of survey techniques. Now there are market researchers working at the studios as well as independent companies specializing in film research. Their goals are the same, though: Determine a statistical picture of the kinds of people who go to movies, find out if certain projects will meet with public favor, and learn how to market films that have already been made.

Determining who might comprise the audience is basically a back-burner project. Since it's not associated with a specific film, its lack of urgency causes it occasionally to get lost in the shuffle. The second function—which movies to make and which movies not to make—is a threat to everyone who makes creative decisions, since it suggests that marketing statistics will in some sense make creative decisions. Still, surveys have been designed to weed out potential losers, and they work like this:

The head of production is considering a package presented to him by a producer. He has doubts because this type of movie is unusual or perhaps because the star has never done this kind of film. He contacts market research to devise a survey. The agencies who perform surveys will then contact between 500 and 1,000 people in four to six cities —some supposedly sophisticated, such as Boston and San Francisco, some supposedly unsophisticated, such as Denver and Des Moines. Only twelve- to forty-nine-year-olds are contacted (moviegoing age groups), either in shopping malls or over the telephone. All but the so-called frequent moviegoers (those attending at least once a month) are then weeded out.

The questions devised by the marketing research department deal with the different ingredients of the film: Would you want to see a film about knights in armor and dragons and trolls? Very much? Some-what? Not at all? A second line of inquiry, given to other respondents, would be about the cast: Would you want to see Robert De Niro and Mariel Hemingway in: A western comedy? A serious drama? A medi-eval fantasy? Finally, still other respondents would be asked how eager they would be to see a medieval fantasy starring Robert De Niro and Mariel Hemingway.

Once the results are analyzed by the head of production, a decision will be made to abort the film, go ahead as planned, or adapt some new strategy, such as recasting. Then again, the results may be totally ignored.

Pretesting is still a fairly uncommon route in filmmaking. More common is the sort of survey that goes on after a film is finished but before it is released. The goal here is to find the advertising approach that works best with the public. Often, the researchers also have to find out how to overcome specific problems of acceptance posed by the film. During the fall of 1979 a company called Associated Film Distribution (AFD) had one of those problems. Marble Arch Productions, their corporate cousin, had just completed a film called *Saturn 3*. In conceiving the project, Marble Arch had quite reasonably accepted the idea that one of the things drawing people into theaters is the name of a star on the marquee. So they hired Farrah Fawcett, along with Kirk Douglas and Harvey Keitel, to star.

At the time, it looked like a fine idea: a good, scary sci-fi yarn featuring a beautiful, popular figure in the entertainment world. How could it miss? An answer to that question came in August. *Saturn 3* had just completed shooting when another film with Ms. Fawcett, *Sunburn*, was released. It bombed, horribly, even embarrassingly. Ms. Fawcett had actively promoted the film, which had only served to identify her even more securely with this fiasco. At the same time, she separated from her husband and dumped her manager, Jay Bernstein. She was beginning to acquire the aura of a loser.

With chilling suddenness a star was no longer a star. She wouldn't draw in the crowds. Worse than that, she might even keep people away. What to do? AFD developed a marketing strategy that accentuated what it thought was the positive (*Saturn 3*'s plot) and downplayed the cast. This approach was developed in part through marketing research.

The research for *Saturn 3* took the form of a five-city survey, conducted in shopping centers during one weekend in late October 1979. The results did not startle anyone at AFD. The respondents were asked just one question about *Saturn 3*: "Would you go see a movie called *Saturn 3*, starring Farrah Fawcett, Kirk Douglas, and Harvey Keitel?" The response to that question, noted Barry Lorie, AFD's vice-president in charge of advertising, publicity, and promotion, was "not terrific, but not bad, either." Still, it was evidently not enthusiastic enough to convince AFD to use the cast as an advertising centerpiece. "The cast is rarely a selling point with this kind of film," claims Lorie, with what seemed like an after-the-fact insight. "Look at *Star Wars*.

And who are Tom Skerritt and Sigourney Weaver?" Lorie asked, referring to two members of the cast of *Alien.*

Not too surprisingly, it was questions about *Alien* and *Star Wars* that comprised the remainder of AFD's marketing survey. Lorie's department was sketching two different advertising themes for the film. One emphasized science fiction hardware and came to be known as the *Star Wars* look. The alternate approach suggested horror with an outer space background, as in *Alien.* When the questionnaires came back to the office, the *Alien* approach won out. According to Lorie, *Alien* had the stronger recognition, stronger than *Star Wars* among respondents who said they weren't big science fiction fans.

The irony in all of this was that Marble Arch had spent a lot of money for a cast that the marketing survey later told them not to advertise. The TV ads neither mentioned nor showed the cast, and nowhere were the actors' names or pictures in evidence in the special *Saturn 3* artwork that decorated the theaters in New York and Los Angeles for the movie's opening run. Three-quarters of a million dollars for Farrah Fawcett (and probably another million for the combined talents of Douglas and Keitel)—and for all the good it did for the marketing of the film, the cast might as well have been unknowns.

One of the principles of movie marketing research is to describe the product as thoroughly as possible to the survey respondents. It follows, then, that one of the most efficient research techniques would be the "sneak preview," since it lets the potential audience actually see the film. Previews were once used to field-test new features. A filmmaker would go to these previews to study how an audience responded to a film. He would look for bad reactions, places where the audience grew restless, and any unintentional humor, and he would then reedit the film. Today, the preview practice is little more than a marketing aid.* The filmmakers don't always attend, reediting is not common, and the expression of the crowd that is taken most seriously is the one that

*Once again, there are exceptions. Reactions by the New York critics to the preview of *Heaven's Gate* caused the film to be yanked from the lucrative Christmas release for extensive repairs.

comes through postcard-size questionnaires viewers are asked to fill out after the movie.

If these cards show unanimous hatred for a film, it will probably be shelved—and then later sold to television. It's best, executives feel, not to throw good advertising money after bad production money. If the audience response is at least mixed, the studio will use the cards to determine if the film should be reedited or, more likely, to figure out how to sell the movie, and to whom. For example, if men especially like a film but women don't, you can bet that ads for it will start cropping up on television during Sunday afternoon football games. If enthusiasm for the film is only moderate, the production company will try to get play dates during the times of the year when competition with potentially more popular films is less fierce.

In some cases previews serve a different purpose. Should a film promise to be an obvious crowd pleaser, the previews are used only to get word of mouth going. Word of mouth—one person telling another about a movie they really liked—is generally considered the most potent, and least manageable, factor in movie marketing. There are other ways of pulling people into theaters, but "good" word of mouth is the surest guarantee of a profit.

Once all the marketing research on behalf of a film is completed, work begins on the formulation of a market position, or selling strategy, for the film. The selling strategy is based around elements in the story line or compelling visual vignettes taken from the completed movie. The strategy at the studios is usually determined in concert by a collection of departments. The marketing department, naturally enough, is compelled by common sense to devise a strategy that maximizes all of the potential publicity value inherent in the story, cast, or even special effects or mammoth budget of a film. Therefore, publicity and promotion will generally be in on the discussions of selling strategy. Distribution, the people who must convince theater owners to play the film, also contribute their thinking.

As in all else in the business of film, things work quite a bit differently with the independent producer/distributors than with the major studios or mini-majors. More often than not, an independent makes the decision to produce a film based on the fact that enough investors are interested in funding the project at hand. After that, little money is left over for sophisticated surveys and most active independents keep themselves in business through pursuing an aggressive policy of "negative pickups," acquiring for distribution already completed films produced outside their company. With negative pickups, the intuition of the person who owns the indie company that the movie will manage to attract an audience—somewhere, somehow—may be the only "marketing" consideration that counts.

Both the studios and the independents merge, though, in their stress on the related publicity and promotion tasks. On the studio side, a minimum of $5 million is committed to launch a new film into the movie marketplace. Though indies cannot afford that sort of promotional price tag, the successful ones among them put as much money as possible into promotional support of their product. As one successful indie owner told us: "The whole value of a film is in how it can be marketed. I don't care how much a film cost to make. That's not its value. Its value is in how well you can convince people to come see it."

Irv Ivers, senior vice-president of advertising, promotion, and publicity at 20th Century-Fox, is assigned the job of convincing people to come see the films produced and distributed by his studio. His description of the piecing together of a selling strategy for *Middle Age Crazy* provides an illustrative example of how it's done at the studios:

"We could have sold the film as the story of a guy who turned forty and suddenly has this midlife crisis and needs to have younger women, and is abdicating his responsibilities to his wife, his son, his mother, and his job. Doesn't sound like a very appealing strategy in today's marketplace.

"You could have done it from the married couple's point of view, Ann-Margret and Bruce Dern, who are going through the midlife crisis, hitting the big four-oh. That too didn't sound like a big enough idea.

"We finally arrived at what we thought was a big idea. We created a campaign that suggested there's a middle-age crazy epidemic and two of the first people to have contracted this disease are Bruce Dern and

Ann-Margret. We tied it all into warning signs, which really came out of the film, about what to look for. Now, that's a much bigger idea."

The "big idea," in Iver's thinking, means finding a common denominator. Instead of making the film seem specialized, the idea is to make it appear to have relevance to the largest possible group of people. For example, instead of trying to sell a film by promoting it as an intimate look at the life of a Broadway director, it's better to say that it's about more generalized subjects, such as "all that music," "all that excitement," "all that glitter," and *All That Jazz*.

Ivers came to 20th after that film had been released but before it had gone into its nationwide run at hundreds of theaters. The "all that glitter" catch phrase had been the cornerstone of the initial strategy. According to Ivers, the film was performing at "a pretty good level, but not terrific." He felt it necessary to develop an even "bigger" idea. "It was perceived by the public as a film that was very sophisticated, a film that was very controversial because of the open heart surgery and the angel-of-death sequences, albeit a film with tremendous artistic value.

"Those perceptions (and we didn't know how deep they went across the country, because it was only playing in four cities) could have had something to do with the 'just okay' performance in those four cities. We felt that we somehow had to broaden the marketplace appeal for the movie. It was perceived as being too sophisticated, and I don't think people really knew what to expect when they saw the film, or really knew what the film was all about.

"So faced with this, and getting ready to broaden the base of *All That Jazz* across the country, getting into perhaps less sophisticated cities when the movie would be broadening out into the suburbs, we rethought an entire strategy for the film.

"Basically, the new strategy had a very *Chorus Line* look to it, where there was this incredible-looking chorus line of what looked like twelve hundred dancers on a stage and a copy line that said, 'Prepare yourself for what goes on before the curtain goes up.' What that copy line says is not merely 'backstage story of a musical,' like *Singin' in the Rain*, but more 'backstage story of *people* in a musical.'

"I think it was important to get across the message that this was a real movie that had a beginning, a middle, and an end, and it was full of not only music but . . . some incredible cinematic feats.

"The television spots really played to that same copy line but started to show some of the production value of the dance numbers and the choreography, some sense of story.

"The things that we did avoid, intentionally, were any mention of his struggles with his health, his death wish, and the open heart surgery. And they were avoided for obvious reasons. They were things people felt uncomfortable about."

The mechanism for getting this positioning out to the public is the purchase of advertising space and television time. Ivers and other marketers say that television is the most effective ad medium. "You can show your product in the same audio-visual form in which it was shot, and it's the widest reaching."

Creation of the actual advertising materials—advertising art for newspapers, magazines, and billboards; television spots; arresting logos —is done by creative teams outside the studios, reflecting an industry-wide pattern of people in creative specialties working on a single-project basis rather than under an employment contract. The studio, as client, approves all art and copy, leaving the details of actual purchase of media space to large, full-service advertising agencies. Independents, because of their tighter cash position, hire the minimum number of people possible for the execution of ad materials. The head of the company may write all the ad copy or put together the television spots. Artists are hired only because the head of the company can't draw, it often seems. And indies would never think of leaving the complex questions of selecting the best stations, the best shows, and the best times for TV ads to others. They deal with the TV stations directly, to insure their message will be heard where and when it will do the most good.

Studios and independents alike rely on a time-honored advertising device, trailers, or "coming attractions," shown in theaters.

"Trailers are the most effective and cost-efficient advertising there is. They have a captive audience. There's nothing like having a darkened theater and a thirty-foot screen for ads. It's a proven audience, and not only that, it's a proven audience at *that* theater," says Peter Koplik. Koplik may be biased. As an employee of National Screen Service, he works for a company whose business is distributing trailers. The first president of the New York–based firm, Herman Robbins, actually invented the trailer. All but a few of the theaters across the country rent their trailers and posters from NSS, at costs ranging from five dollars to fifty dollars a week, depending on theater size and location.

Trailers used to be turned out by a division of the editing department at each studio. Then, when the production drought of the 1960s hit, the in-house trailer departments were scrapped as part of an austerity program. Independent trailer producers—many of whom had been recently cut from the studio squads—stepped in to fill the vacuum on the theory that lower overhead and competitive bidding would turn out more effective film for less money. Current practices foster an intense rivalry among these independents, who are awarded contracts one trailer at a time.

How are themes for trailers developed? Don Enright, an independent trailer producer who has made trailers for such action pictures as *Shoot*, *Good Guys Wear Black*, *Gentle Savage*, and *Search and Destroy*, offered this explanation: "My editor and I project the film once and make notes on what we think we can use. We come up with a concept, get that approved, order the scenes we've selected, and then just refine it and refine it and refine it more. We get it approved, add narration, sound effects, music, then get it approved again by the distributor, and often the producer as well."

Enright adds that the typical trailer job "takes about three weeks of your time, spread over about a month," an estimate other trailer makers echo. "Then comes the real pain. You need the negative of the picture to make the trailer from, but the producer needs the neg to make prints with so he can get his product into the theaters. The distributor is yelling at you to get the trailer done; the producer is yelling that you can't have the neg."

Insuring that the finished trailer will best show off the film it is promoting, Enright and his colleagues bring a number of approaches into play. Trailers for action pictures generally cram as much mayhem as possible into three minutes of film. "Usually you have enough action in the film that it's no problem," Enright claims.

Even a great trailer won't bring in any business if no one sees it. As effective as trailers seem to be, they're not always utilized to their fullest potential. In theory they should be shown throughout the run of the preceding film, but in many cases theaters will book a film without knowing what their next film will be. Theater owners, then, are hesitant to plug a film that may end up in another theater. Also, there seems to be a resistance on the part of at least some members of the audience to seeing trailers—or, as they conceive of them, advertising they've had to pay to see. So some films, in their more prestigious runs, don't appear with trailers. *Apocalypse Now* is one example.

Sometimes, a producer or studio will splice a trailer for their next film onto one that's currently on the screen. It's a fairly shrewd move, but one that meets resistance from theater owners because, again, they don't like to advertise films that aren't necessarily going to play at their theater. Out come the scissors.

Finally, a lot of trailers miss their audience because they're simply not projected, since it's a lot of trouble for projectionists to thread up a projector for a mere three minutes or so of running time, and then to reload. As a result, in some theaters, trailers sit around gathering dust.

That trailers are taken so lightly even by exhibitors is still more proof of the existence of a fragmented film audience. It hasn't been since the early 1950s that people went regularly to the same neighborhood theater, no matter what was playing. Today, it is often said, people don't leave the house to go to the movies; they leave to see a specific film. The theater owners know this, which may explain why they are so cavalier about showing trailers. Most of them believe that there will be very little overlap between the audience for film A and the one for film B. Someone who attended film A is more likely to be watching television at home next week than to be at the theater seeing film B.

Ironically, it is this fact of modern life—the potency of television —that has become central to the effective marketing of movies. Just twenty years ago, the movie business was by and large only beginning to wake up to the realization that TV was here to stay. Today television is the cornerstone of marketing. Studios and indies routinely place advertisements in the trade papers to announce a "media blitz" on behalf of a current film project. The blitz may involve saturation advertising in magazines and newspapers, huge billboards featuring the distinctive logo designed for the film, even searchlights at the opening in the grand Hollywood tradition. But without talk show appearances for the cast and TV coverage of the film, the blitz is grounded. One studio marketer told us that a feature about the star of a just-released film on ABC's popular "20/20" is worth upward of $20 million in advertising. He admits that he was around in the days when television was viewed as little more than an upstart. But, he adds, "these are different days."

14

MERCHANDISING

THIS IS A STORY THAT BEGINS OUTSIDE OF THE FILM INDUSTRY AND involves an often-exploited minority, children. It's the story of *Urban Cowboy* western shirts, *The Empire Strikes Back* Dixie Cups, *Star Trek* hamburgers, and a host of other items and schemes, which now make up a multimillion-dollar subindustry within the film business: merchandising.

Until the mid 1970s, movies were the poor cousins of television when it came to merchandising. Sound tracks and books (novelizations) had always brought income to producers and studios, but the manufacturers who bought licenses to make other kinds of products such as toys or T-shirts figured that regular weekly exposure on television was the key to selling their goods. This theory was no doubt formed during the mid 1950s, when Davy Crockett's weekly appearances on the Disney TV show made coonskin caps de rigueur for millions of children. Later, more proof came with successful products based on cartoon shows. In comparison, movies seemed to be quick, one-shot affairs, not around long enough to sustain a product in the marketplace. All that changed with *Star Wars*.

The phenomenal success of most of the scores of *Star Wars* items showed that all sorts of products could ride on the coattails of a hit film. It also showed that through shrewd merchandising, a studio could make millions of dollars above and beyond income from movie theaters.

The studios tend to define merchandising as being any instance of an outside company using a film title, or an image from a film, on a product or as part of an advertising campaign. This latter case is called a tie-in, and as its name suggests, it is a partnership of two different companies in a unified advertising strategy.

When filmmakers engage in merchandising, they are either selling or bartering an affiliation with their films. Sometimes the manufacturers approach the studios, but in other instances it's the studios that mount aggressive campaigns to sell licenses to their films. In either case, it's worth noting the considerations on the manufacturer's side. First, he faces competition. If his pair of shoes has the words *Star Wars* on it, they might stand out against his competition. Second, almost any movie that's released by a studio is going to have a national advertising and publicity campaign, involving the expenditure of millions of dollars in all media. Billboards will be everywhere. So will television commercials. Filmgoers will see previews for the film in movie theaters. The stars will show up on talk shows and in the newspapers. All of this promotional activity helps to sell products associated with the film.

In return for the rights to sell a product centered around a film, the manufacturer must pay money to the owner of the film. He may pay a licensing fee, royalties (usually with a guaranteed minimum), or a combination of the two. The most paid up front for such a license is in the neighborhood of $100,000, while the royalty is usually around 10 percent of the retail price of the item being manufactured.

The businessman who is considering paying $10,000 to put a movie logo on underwear that would serve the same purpose undecorated is taking a considerable risk. Even if the film is successful, his product won't necessarily grab the public's fancy. If the film bombs, it will almost certainly take his line of underwear with it. One week of ads for the movie, and that could be it. Yet if he waits to see how the film will do before buying a license, someone else might snare the underwear license, or the licensing fee could be raised up out of his reach. Some companies have been known to purchase a license and then not manufacture anything until the film has proven itself in theaters. That way, if the film fails, all that is lost is the licensing fee, not the cost of making the product. As compensation for the risks attendant to licensing (and the cost of the license), manufacturers build a little extra profit into their merchandise. *Star Wars* watches, for example, cost $12, but the same watches, unadorned, were only $10.

This, of course, leads to the question of just who are the targets of merchandising. The answer, in large part, is children. First, because so many of the items that are geared to merchandising fall into the category of toys and novelties, and second, because children aren't known for making the kind of cost-versus-quality judgments that would lead them to opt for the $10 watch instead of the $12 *Star Wars* watch.

Proof of the impact of these consumers can be seen in the studios' employment of executives who do nothing but coordinate merchandising. In addition to deciding who gets licenses and negotiating the deals, the merchandiser is often a salesman as well, going to outside companies in an effort to sell licenses. His goal is not primarily money. According to the filmmakers, money is secondary to promotional value in a merchandising deal.

But, even though money is officially assigned this secondary role, the revenue from successful merchandising deals obviously can't be ignored. Merchandising arrangements, when they couple a successful film with a popular product, can generate millions of dollars of profit for the studios. Besides, one toy company executive pointed out, if money were not important, studios wouldn't spend so much time arguing over half a percentage point of potential profit in the royalty contract. And they do.

Once the royalties come in, the money can be used to help pay back the cost of making the film or go directly to the producer and/or the studio. Still another slice of the pie goes to whoever has original story credit, a rule specified by the Writers Guild. Much of the time, however, the pie is not a very big one. *Star Wars* brought an estimated $20 million in royalties and licensing fees to its studio and its producers, but this is clearly an extreme case.

To the producers, merchandising is a risk within a risk, because most films simply cannot be merchandised, and, among those that can be, only a few will be hits. So it's no surprise when the merchandisers say that revenue is less important than promotional value.

But how important is that value? Is it so important that the studios might sometimes actually pay a manufacturer to merchandise products? The answer is a quick and unanimous no from the filmmakers, but that's not to say the manufacturers don't ask. A merchandiser at Disney complained that the single biggest problem he had was what he called ignorance. "They [the manufacturers] just don't understand the value they're getting. They say, 'Hey, look at all the advertising we're giving you.' They just don't understand." The studios seem to be saying that financing movies is enough of a risk for them; no sense spending even more money to subsidize someone else's business. The film company's collective ego may be involved in this, too; it's almost a point of honor that the cash must never flow outward, to the manufacturers. Some of the producers, however, have been known to give licenses away when their films did not look like commercial contenders.

The law works in the field of commercial tie-ins, too, but often minus the cash. Instead, outside companies who use movie references in ads for their own products will barter for the use of copyrighted material. What they have to offer is ad space—exposure for the film. They'll buy a specified number of ads in specified media, in exchange for the use of film-related material that would appear in those ads.

As the studios see it, this is a sensible way to acquire additional advertising. From the point of view of the companies (often soft drink manufacturers, fast food chains, and others doing business with children), there is the accepted belief that identification with a hit movie will give the company that much more of an edge on its competition. Retailers—often large department stores—know that they can sometimes get free tie-ins with newly released films. Shoppers don't seem to mind being confronted with this type of unexpected advertising, and the stores are more than happy to hype a sale of, say, cowboy-related clothing, with a few posters of John Travolta in *Urban Cowboy*.

These tie-ins are usually conceived by the studios' merchandising offices but are occasionally the ideas of the manufactuers or stores. In most cases, the lines of communication have been opened long before; the merchandisers at the studios have a vast network of contacts among manufacturers and retailers.

When a tie-in is arranged, the stores need advertising art, often in the form of posters or life-size, freestanding cardboard cutouts of the movies' characters. These are provided by the studio, either dealing directly with stores across the country or through local ad agencies, engaged for that purpose.

A tie-in deal may involve an up-front payment or a "trade-out," as was the case with a Disney-Pepsi tie-in. In this instance, Pepsi made an initial payment to Disney and then guaranteed that a like amount would be spent in advertising. The contract then made stipulations about the size and quantity of the ads.

As it is in so many other ways, Disney is a special case when it comes to merchandising. It's clear that this is one studio that doesn't use merchandising for just its promotional value; it makes a great deal of money from merchandising and tie-ins. Requests pour daily into the studio for licenses to an unbelievable range of products, and even that is not enough for Disney, for it also employs a corps of salesmen throughout the country whose job it is to find companies to merchandise Disney products.

Another purpose these personnel serve is to scour the country—and the world—looking for copyright infringements. The infringements may be as innocuous as the corner bakery painting Mickey Mouse's portrait in icing on their cakes or as significant as counterfeit Mickey Mouse watches, but either way the company must stop it. Disney is obligated to stop such infringements, not necessarily to protect the consumer, but instead to protect their own copyrights, since a copyright that is not firmly enforced by its holder can sometimes be terminated by the courts.

Part of the reason for Disney's success in merchandising is its perpetual annuity in the form of its cartoon characters. As long as there are children, it seems unlikely that Mickey and Minnie Mouse, Donald Duck, Pluto, or Goofy will ever stop earning money for Disney. It's estimated that these and other characters—not tied to any particular film—constitute 80 percent of Disney's merchandising business, while new films make up the remaining 20 percent.

A central merchandising theory generated by the Disney characters and, also, by *Star Wars* is that to appeal to children, films must contain colorful, often exaggerated characters. Without such characters merchandising is next to impossible.

A closely related theory is the concept of collectability, an idea that preys on children's compulsiveness, whether in the form of trading cards, toy figurines, or mugs. "Get *all* the *Star Wars* figurines . . . or, start your collection of *The Empire Strikes Back* glasses *now*!" The implication is that a kid has somehow failed as a human being if his collection is anything less than complete. Even if the film does have a memorable character or two, that still won't be enough to make it a merchandising success; there should be enough to support a line of collectibles.

When there are a lot of interesting characters, the toy companies have their young clientele over the proverbial barrel. Unlike adults, children are not comparison shoppers. They don't have to be, since few of them are confronted with the daily realities of budgeting their resources. In addition, they tend to be more brand-name-oriented than adults, so much so that model spaceship "A," which to the casual adult observer is a near duplicate of model spaceship "B," is totally different from B to the child . . . and totally unacceptable. The result of all this is that the child who wants a Luke Skywalker action figure will accept no substitutes. And, since Luke Skywalker falls under a copyright, only one company can manufacture the figure—a virtual monopoly. The toy companies are not unaware of these considerations when they set prices for their products.

One example of how all this works is in the area of dolls—called "large action figures" rather than dolls by the toy industry, since these are items designed for boys as well as girls. The dolls are made of molded plastic and stand about a foot tall. Different companies manufacture different characters, and some have reached pretty deeply into the barrel to find heroes and villains. One company, for example, sells a doll that is the likeness of one Oscar Goldman, a man in a business suit, who has no super powers but who happens to be the boss and mentor of TV's Six Million Dollar Man. He can be had for about $13.

Trying to originate their own science fiction line (a move that makes licensing fees unnecessary), the Ideal Toy Company created Star Team. The two most prominent members of Star Team are a black-clad warrior and a golden robot, both of which bear distinct resemblances to *Star Wars* characters. Aside from the lack of a movie tie-in (no small deficit), the main difference, it seems, was their original price —about $5 less than the competition. But even that was not enough to make the dolls a success. The Star Team ended its life on the toy shelves marked down to $3.99, with few takers.

The same principle applies to the smaller figures, too. These are three to four inches tall with limbs and heads that usually swivel. Less detailed figures—slightly smaller toy soldiers or cowboys and Indians —are still relatively inexpensive: They come ten to the package for about $1.50. These, of course, are generic, unlicensed figures, molded in one piece and unpainted. The *Star Wars* figures, as well as two competing lines, the Micronauts and the Shogun Warriors, are sold one at a time, and feature movable and/or detachable parts and some hand painting. As a result, their per-unit prices vary from $2, for the cheapest Micronauts (which have no movie connection) and the Shoguns (which appear on Japanese television), all the way up to $3.25, for the *Star Wars* and *Flash Gordon* figures. At first glance, the products seem roughly equal, despite the 60-percent variation in price. On further examination, the Micronauts and, to a lesser extent, the Shoguns appear the better bargain. Unlike the more expensive figures from *Star Wars* and *Flash Gordon*, these two lines trade on the principle of interchangeability: Parts from one figure can be used to alter imaginatively the appearance of any of the other robotlike creatures in the line. The *Star Wars* figures just stand there.

Because that's all they do, the *Star Wars* characters might be said to have a high degree of specificity, in contrast to something like a large, empty carton that kids could sit in and play in. The carton could be a race car one day, a cavalry fort the next, and even a spaceship, depending on the child's imagination. Luke Skywalker is always Luke Skywalker, a potential victim of its youthful owner's notoriously short attention span.

Kenner, the *Star Wars* action figures' manufacturer, seems to have taken into account the boredom factor, if not actually having fueled it. The less a figure can do, the sooner the child will lose interest, and the sooner the child loses interest, the sooner he will want another figure. At last count there were over thirty of the small figures from both *Star Wars* and *The Empire Strikes Back.* Characters who had been on-screen for only a few seconds were immortalized in plastic—at $3.25 a shot—and there were even second editions of the three main characters, since they wore different costumes in the sequel. Perhaps the most telling *Star Wars* merchandise is a simple black vinyl-covered box, about one foot by nine inches by four inches. Inside, there are plastic subdividers, as in a cash register, dividing the box into neat rows of squares. Aside from those dividers, the box is empty. Outside, on the lid, is a collage of *Star Wars* photos and the information that this box was designed as a holder for *Star Wars* figures. Each time the owner of one of these boxes opens it, he is reminded how many characters he still needs to buy in order to complete the set. This box costs $9, with no figures included.

Despite occasional merchandising failures, the studios have remained bullish on the field, and not just for kids' films and gimmick movies (which might yield items like the toy sharks from *Jaws* or the alien figurines from *Close Encounters* and *Alien*). Conceding that his job depended in large part on accurately assessing the likes and dislikes of children, Paramount executive director of merchandising and licensing, Hy Foreman, went on to show a step-by-step merchandising outline—one that he had most recently used for *Urban Cowboy.*

Foreman had a list of generic products designed as a sort of grid to match up with movies. The products, which numbered in the hundreds, were by no means all geared to children. Everything from men's suits to gelatin was listed—anything that could have a movie name imprinted somewhere on it or on its container. Note, too, that all the products existed long before the film; it's a rare (but lucrative) thing when a movie creates a product that has never before been seen in the marketplace, as was the case with the *Star Wars* figurines and the rubber *Jaws* sharks. Most of the time, though, merchandising is a matter of emblazoning Flash Gordon's picture on bed sheets and towels or selling the *Urban Cowboy* name to lines of boots and western shirts.

Once Foreman goes through his master list to see what products would constitute appropriate merchandising for the film at hand, his next step is to contact companies. According to Foreman, there are only certain companies that buy licenses, so the field is somewhat narrowed, although the really successful films tend to bring small, unknown companies out of the woodwork in search of licenses. Depending on how hot his property is, Foreman either takes what he can get or sits back and lets the bids come in.

The bids, of course, involve more than money; they also contain advertising strategies and the expected assurances of high quality in the finished product. In these two areas the studios have been known to be very picky. Obviously they don't want their films associated with shoddy workmanship, but less obviously they are legally obligated to enforce a host of credit requirements in advertisements as one of their responsibilities to the talent. If, for example, the director's name must appear with an apostrophe-*s* after it above the name of the film, then it must appear that way on the coloring book as well as on the screen. Or, if the two stars of the film have contracts that stipulate equal co-billing, then their names must reflect that on model kits, too. The merchandisers, the manufacturer, and even some studio lawyers are kept busy making sure credit agreements are carried out to the letter. Additionally, the studios usually have the right of approval on product artwork. "You wouldn't believe some of the terrible likenesses you see," Foreman noted.

The interesting thing about the *Urban Cowboy* merchandising campaign was that the Delta Boot Company's ad was propped up against a file cabinet in Foreman's office, waiting for approval a month *after* the film's release. Foreman was tight-lipped about Paramount's deal with Delta, but it seemed clear that this very adult film (which was rated "PG") did not seem to have much merchandising potential prior to its release. Otherwise, the merchandise would have been on the shelves to coincide with the release of the film. *Star Wars* was released in the spring of 1977, and its success took the manufacturers by surprise—so much so that the tiny *Star Wars* figurines weren't ready to go on sale until the beginning of the next year. Kenner marked Christmas 1977 by selling gift certificates, redeemable for the figurines when they were ready, a month or two later.

Largely because of that embarrassing and well-publicized spectacle, the manufacturers have become a lot more sophisticated about movie merchandising. These days, it's not surprising to see toy companies dealing with the studios and producers when their films are still in the script stage. A representative of Mattel said that he looks for "high adventure" and "attractive protagonists, or characters that are particularly ugly or threatening" in the scripts he reads. It should be noted, though, that the scripts are submitted only to see if the toy companies are interested in licenses; the filmmakers don't want any creative input from the toy makers.

Also becoming more sophisticated about merchandising are the film producers. In 1976 Charles Lippincott hired on as publicist for *Star Wars* during its production. Later, thanks to the impetus that *Star Wars* gave his career, he became an independent marketing consultant. His efforts in publicity led to him acting as a clearinghouse for the *Star Wars* merchandising. One problem he had was in determining which companies would be sold the licenses. Because the film had not yet been released, it was not a seller's market.

"When I went to talk to Revell about *Star Wars*, they hassled back and forth for, oh, a month and a half or two months, and they decided not to go with it, because they didn't think it would be a big hit. They didn't know how to evaluate it.

"Mego just about physically tossed me out of the office when I presented *Star Wars.*" (However, the company later reversed its stand. Too late, Lippincott noted gleefully.)

Another consideration was quality control, since inferior toys reflect on the movie.

"When I went through *Star Wars,* I went to Toys-R-Us and took a notebook and wrote down [notes]. . . . I checked up on what was going on. I looked at tags, I looked at 'Star Trek,' I looked at a lot of different stuff. I looked at toy companies, the quality of toys, things like that, and I talked to people. When I went to the San Diego Comicon of 1976, I asked about model kits and talked to a number of the kids. I asked them what model kits were the best, things like that. A lot of kids are never asked these questions. People just go and make deals. They think, 'So-and-so's offering a lot of money; I'm going to go with their model kits.' But if they make terrible kits, it's gonna reflect on your image. That kid's gonna write in and say, 'I bought the *Millennium Falcon* and so-and-so piece is missing,' and he writes in and he gets no action at all. And he has this *Millennium Falcon* kit he can't complete. It's gonna piss the kid off."

It's Lippincott's apparent belief that successful merchandising lies in being a sort of ombudsman for the children who buy the toys. That means thinking like one, and, said Lippincott, most merchandisers just aren't "adult-looking kids, like me."

15

RECOGNITION:

HOW MUCH
IS THAT OSCAR ON
THE MANTLE?

FOR NINE MONTHS OUT OF EVERY YEAR, THE WORD "GOOD" USUALLY means just one thing in the film business: commercially successful. If a film performs well in the marketplace, it is good.

All that supposedly changes during the months between December and mid April. That is Oscar time, when the moviemakers get down to the serious business of rewarding artistry . . . and if you believe that, you'll be glad to know that D. W. Griffith was just signed to direct the next *Star Wars* sequel.

Just the word "Oscar" is a big commercial draw. It has brought high ratings to the annual awards telecast, which in turn has led individual networks to pay millions of dollars to the Academy of Motion Picture Arts and Sciences for the rights to televise the ceremony. The huge TV audience means that every nominee gets some very valuable free advertising.

Oscars, and even nominations, can help careers, too, although it's been pointed out that many of the winners for best acting simply drift into obscurity with their statuettes. In the technical areas, though (sound, editing, special effects, and so on), an Oscar will almost always mean that the recipient can raise his asking price. And not all actors suffer the Oscar "curse." Meyer Mishkin, an agent whose clients have included Lee Marvin (Best Actor, *Cat Ballou*, 1965) and Richard Dreyfuss (Best Actor, *The Goodbye Girl*, 1977), estimated in 1979 that a Best Actor Oscar lets an agent tack on an additional $250,000 when negotiating his client's next role.

A Best Picture Oscar or any of the other major Academy Awards —or even a nomination—usually means a lucrative rerelease for the film, as was the case with *Annie Hall*. That film came out in the spring of 1977, did its business, and didn't resurface until Oscar time, almost a year later. Once it got back into the theaters, it grossed twice as much as it did the first time out, without the benefit of an extensive new advertising campaign. Some in the industry have estimated that a Best Picture Oscar can add as much as $10 million to a film's gross.

Fair enough: an instance of people going to see good movies. Yet these movies won't get Oscars unless considerable money is spent campaigning for the awards. There is a yearly discussion in Hollywood about whether an Oscar can be bought by staging elaborate, expensive campaigns for them. The answer usually arrived at is no, but, as with any political campaign, money must be spent, even though spending it is not a guarantee of winning.

The rules of the competition are simple. Three thousand five hundred members of the Academy first nominate, then choose, winners in categories familiar to anyone who's seen the telecast. The membership of the Academy is a who's who of filmmaking, with entrance hinging on member recommendations and a vote by the specific branch. Among the branches are the actors, directors, cinematographers, writers, and, somewhat surprisingly, executives and public relations people. In branches that do not award an Oscar, the members only help nominate best picture. When it comes time to *vote* for the actual awards, however, every member of the Academy is entitled to vote in every category. Do art directors know anything about acting? Do cinematographers know about music? Do sound men know much about editing? Probably as much as anyone else. But not much more.

To influence this somewhat quirky electoral process, studios, producers, distributors, and even the talent themselves spend an amount that totals hundreds of thousands of dollars every year. Academy rules prohibit electioneering, but for all practical purposes this is usually defined very narrowly as a ban on person-to-person solicitation of votes.

Money is linked to the Oscar in one other crucial way: A film cannot lose at the box office and then win on Oscar night. There's no rule demanding this, but in Hollywood, nothing provokes partial amnesia faster than a film that has died at the box office. As a result, nominees tend to come from the ranks of the highest grossers.

If commercial success and the Oscar go hand in hand, what would happen if the order were switched around, with the Oscar coming first and the film going into general release later? Would the Oscar guarantee success to a film that was about to go into general release?

That's what a handful of executives at Universal were wondering in the summer of 1978, when they considered the impending release of a film they were distributing, *The Deer Hunter.* At three hours long, with an unconventional narrative structure, *The Deer Hunter* had one other thing about it that made its chances for success seem dubious: Much of it was set in the Vietnam War, the war the American public supposedly wanted to forget.

All these factors left the executives at Universal not knowing quite how to market the film. Enter Alan Carr. Carr first came to public attention in the late 1960s as the personal manager of Ann-Margret. A portly easterner, Carr wallowed in the gaudiest trappings and traditions of old Hollywood until he became somewhat of a celebrity himself. Later, his knack for hyperbolic promotion helped turn a film he produced, *Grease,* into one of the all-time box office winners. It was the success of that film that made Universal seek after his opinions. Carr's only other connection to *The Deer Hunter* was that he had a deal to produce a film for EMI, the same company that financed *The Deer Hunter.*

Carr's recollections display an uncommonly healthy ego, but his words also illustrate the vast chasm that sometimes exists between the kind of lives we see in the movies and the life-styles of the people who make them:

"I was sitting in my cabana drinking champagne. I had *Grease* about to make $100 million, movie offers from every studio, and a fund-raising dinner for Governor Brown coming up at my house when Barry Spikings [*The Deer Hunter*'s producer] asked me to see it.

"I knew I wouldn't like it. It's about two things I don't care about: Vietnam and poor people, directed by this guy [Michael] Cimino, who I remember directing Ann-Margret in Canada Dry ads five years ago. Three hours of Pittsburgh steelworkers. I'm not going to like it," Carr figured.

Finally, on July 14, 1978, Carr, after "lunch at my hangout Ma Maison," went to see the film "for friendship reasons.

"I'm a half-hour late and I'm the only one there. So the picture starts. By the middle of the movie, I was crying so hard I had to go to the men's room to put cold water on my face. And again at the end. I'm having dinner for Governor Brown that night at my house, and I'm truly emotionally undone. I apologize to the governor, whom I had never met, and say I have been affected by this film so deeply I cannot speak." The governor's reaction was not mentioned by Carr.

The next day Carr was invited to a meeting at Universal. He was asked a simple question: Could *The Deer Hunter* bring in the box office?

"I sensed right away this is an event movie," Carr said. "It's not *Grease*, where it's ninety minutes, in-out, and turn over the grosses. Audiences will have to be educated that it's not a case of get a baby-sitter, eat popcorn, and dance around the theater."

From that moment on, Carr claimed, "It was all a plan. I convinced them [Universal] that they had to open the movie out of town, in Chicago or Detroit. L.A. is jaded and spoiled by the movies. At previews in Westwood, they cheer for Telly Savalas chasing an airplane."

Carr set up a screening for two directors, Steven Spielberg and Vincente Minnelli, who symbolized differing age and artistic factions in the directing community. Although Carr wasn't saying, it seems clear that he was gambling that their positive word of mouth would help get *The Deer Hunter* a Best Director Award from the Directors Guild of America.

The Directors Guild of America is a body unrelated to the Academy, although there is some common membership. The Guild is the union for directors and assistant directors, and therefore almost all directors are members. Only the most prominent directors get into the director's branch of the Academy, however. Once they become members of the Academy, their major yearly duty is to nominate five directors for the Best Directing Oscar.

After the Oscar nominees are made public but before the winners are announced, the DGA's membership single out their own director of the year.

Although DGA spokesman Joe Youngerman claimed the announcement of the DGA award is coincidental—"Our timing is like that because we have less rigamarole than the Academy and we like to have our awards dinner around Saint Patrick's Day"—it's hard to discount the notion that the DGA vote is meant to influence the Academy. In about 90 percent of the Oscar ceremonies since the late 1950s, the DGA-named Best Director has seen his film take the Best Picture Oscar. This fact is usually pointed out in the trade papers when the DGA announces its winner. The DGA eventually gave their 1978 award to Cimino.

After *The Deer Hunter* was screened for Minnelli and Spielberg, Carr convinced Universal to hold back the movie from its scheduled general release in September. He wanted to aim instead for a limited-engagement year-end run on both coasts, the minimum needed to qualify the movie for Oscar eligibility in 1978.

"I said, 'If we can't sell out Westwood and the Coronet [in New York] with this film for one week, I'm leaving the business,' " Carr recalled.

"I knew it would be the Christmas cocktail party subject in New York. Everybody would be asking if you saw it, were you one of the five hundred people who saw one of the eight shows? They said I shouldn't give a film to New York and take it away. I said that's how you treat New Yorkers."

In Westwood, according to Carr, "It was pandemonium. People were calling, Nureyev, Betty Bacall, asking for house seats, but there were no house seats. We were saving the film for the Academy" (whose membership cards entitled them to free admission for themselves and just one guest).

Only one VIP screening was arranged, hosted by EMI board chairman Lord Bernard Delfont. "We had no party, though," Carr said, "just drinks and finger food before, because everybody had worked that day and it's a long film. You don't want to party after this film, you want to get in your car and go home."

By then it was the end of the year, time for the nominations and awards. As in most Oscar campaigns, Universal mounted a two-pronged assault on the voters, through advertisements in the trade newspapers and screenings for Academy members.

A large share of Universal's $250,000 *Deer Hunter* Oscar campaign budget was eaten up by a sophisticated print advertising campaign designed exclusively for people in the movie industry, a campaign the general public never saw.

Just before the opening of the film, a lavishly illustrated supplement, the first of three, appeared in *Daily Variety* and the *Hollywood Reporter*, listing only the screen credits for the film and excerpts from positive reviews. The second insert in the series bore the antlers and parachute logo of the movie in red ink on the cover and announced the eleven nomination categories that *The Deer Hunter* sought. Again, critical reaction and lots of photos were the hallmarks of the piece.

Once *The Deer Hunter* got its nominations, another insert was published in the trades, listing the nine categories in which the film had been nominated, and stressing the critical praise. In addition, a two-page collage of trade paper headlines told of the film's healthy box office business.

Not only did the insert approach enable the movie to get its message across in a self-contained format without competition from ads for other movies, but each insert also did double duty as a mailing piece to Academy members. Universal also used the mailboxes of the voting membership to encourage them to come to any of the scheduled studio screenings of the film.

Once the nominations have been announced, the Academy sponsors a random drawing of screening times for the various studios. It's done that way so that screenings of the nominated films won't conflict with one another. Until *The Deer Hunter*'s success, most studios didn't use all their allotted opportunities to show their films, either out of general disorganization or because they were relying on other venues. Universal used all of its screening opportunities.

In concert with the move to draw Academy members to the screenings, Universal assigned a full-time staffer to the task of keeping tabs on how many voters had shown their Academy cards to see the film. The week before the final ballots were even mailed out, Universal logs showed that more than 2,400 of the 2,700 L.A. voters had seen the movie.

Perhaps the biggest—and, in retrospect, smartest—gamble that Carr and Universal took was in this area. The most basic philosophy of an Oscar campaign is to get the film seen by as many of the 3,500 voting Academy members as possible. Incredibly, Academy members are under no obligation to see all, or even any, of the nominated movies before voting. The assumption the campaigners work under, then, is that members will not vote for films they haven't seen. Hence, the importance of screenings.

Another way of exposing nominated films is to put them on pay TV in Los Angeles. At first glance the spectacle of a rival medium playing the kingmaker in the Oscar race is difficult to comprehend. What allowance does the tube make for wide screen, or stereo sound, or 70-millimeter cinematography? And yet, there is no rule against Academy members voting for cinematography or sound based on what they've seen at home on TV.

At the same time, the economics of the TV showings are hard to argue with. Studios want their nominees to be seen. Pay TV wants to show the nominees, not because they necessarily want to provide a service for the Academy, but rather because they want to provide a service for their general subscribers—and, not so incidentally, to attract new subscribers. By showing the nominees and, before that, the *potential* nominees (as judged by their studios), the pay channels get to show the hottest films of the preceding year for a full three months. That's a potent lure to new subscribers.

It's clearly a mutually advantageous situation, but it's more advantageous to the pay TV companies because the films usually come to them free. With only a few thousand theater admissions to lose, the studios often give L.A.'s pay TV channels their movies for a few showings in hopes of reaching Academy members. Under normal circumstances, of course, pay TV pays the studios for the films it shows. At Oscar time, however, the channels sell a product that hasn't cost them anything.

With little embarrassment, executives now plan part of their Oscar campaigns around cable screenings. The thought of seeing films at commercial theaters with the paying public seems almost alien to many members of the Academy, even though that activity provides movie people with their livelihood.

Maybe it has to be that way because of L.A.'s geography—and its people. The 2,700 Academy voters living in Los Angeles are an elite group at the top of a glamorous industry. They've got money and influence, and the last thing many of them want is to brave the crowds in tiny, congested Westwood Village, the city-within-a-city that has almost all of L.A.'s first-run theaters. As for second-run neighborhood theaters, to go to one of those might be a sign of diminished personal status. Add in the fact that excepting Beverly Hills, the wealthy tend to live in the more isolated areas of the city, such as Malibu, the canyons, and the Hollywood Hills, and an evening in front of the tube shapes up as a convenient way of catching the Oscar contenders.

Universal didn't agree. In 1979 they were the only major company that didn't give its nominees to pay TV. By not televising *The Deer Hunter,* Universal succeeded in making its viewing more of an "event," in line with Carr's strategy. Since it was not widely available in theaters, a ticket to a studio screening became a status symbol. As for the hassle of gassing up the car and driving down out of the hills into Universal City—there were rewards for that, too. Unlike regular theaters, studio screenings offer all of the following: free, convenient parking; guaranteed seating; quiet and generally respectful fellow viewers; no trash on the floor; no waiting line. In short, screening audiences are treated with the deference that they might sorely miss at commercial theaters.

Universal's party-line excuse for not televising their nominees is that production values are lost on the tube. That's true, of course, but something else is lost on TV: emotional impact. On a wry little film such as *Annie Hall*, that's not much of a factor, but on *The Deer Hunter*, it clearly was. For many in the Academy, the 1978 Best Picture voting (which took place in March 1979) was between several TV shows—and one movie. *The Deer Hunter* was that movie; it won five Academy Awards, including Best Picture. The day after the Oscars, Universal paid for a two-page ad in the trades thanking Alan Carr.

Whether it's a race for Best Picture, Best Actor, or any of the other awards, the losers always outnumber the winners. Sometimes the story of what went wrong turns out to be as interesting as what went right.

In summer 1979 Avco-Embassy distributed a film called *The Onion Field*, based on Joseph Wambaugh's best-seller. Wambaugh had acted as executive producer on the film and had written the screenplay as well. He had even raised the money needed to make the film from his wealthy neighbors in San Marino, California.

An emotionally wrenching true story, *The Onion Field* was not a great popular success, but it did garner a sizable cache of favorable reviews. Those reviews set the people at Avco to work on an Oscar campaign. Part of their motivation was money, of course. If the film won a major award or two, they figured, there would be some rerelease income. But there was something else, too, something peculiar to Avco: the need for prestige.

When Avco's executives took a look back, all they saw was a brief, lackluster history. Sure, they distributed and occasionally produced, but they had no back lot, few big hits, and no memories of any golden age of moviemaking. The people at Avco saw themselves as being a little like poor relations. Worse, many filmmakers shared that perception.

Our source at Avco cited the film *Meatballs* as an example of being stung by low prestige. *Meatballs* was independently made in Canada on a very low budget and was later shown to a number of studios in hopes of arranging a distribution deal. Avco was one of the studios interested: "That would have been a perfect film for us to distribute," our source said. "We could have done a lot with it." But the producer made a deal with more prestigious Paramount instead. "They said they had to, and I could see their point," the source ruefully concluded.

An Oscar—recognition for Avco in front of millions of TV viewers —would have been a good first step toward gaining some respect. But for which Oscar would they campaign? In strategy sessions the Avco executives decided Joseph Wambaugh's screenplay and James Woods's performance had the best chances of being nominated. Since the film was based on a book, the trade ads promoting Wambaugh would do so in the category of Best Screenplay Adapted from Another Medium.

James Woods, one of the stars of the film, was a little harder to categorize. It was Woods's portrayal of murderer Greg Powell that gave Avco's executives their highest hopes. There was little question in the minds of Avco's executives that the actor could make a good run at an Oscar, but they weren't sure which Oscar: Best Actor or Best Supporting Actor?

Due to the documentarylike structure of the film, the roles were hard to define. John Savage was top-billed, as a policeman who barely escapes death at the hands of Woods's character. The film traces the policeman's life through the ordeal and into the years beyond it. At the same time, it follows Woods through the crime, the trials, and into prison. Since the two actors' on-screen times are about the same, the traditional distinctions between lead and supporting players are inoperative. So, the people at Avco based their decision on factors outside the film. Woods, said one worker in Avco's special projects division, was a new kid on the block, a New York actor who hadn't been around that long, yet who enjoyed credibility from past roles. Such things aren't supposed to matter to the voters, who are told to consider only the performance and not a total career when they cast their ballots; but Avco tried to be a little more realistic about the matter. Their final consideration was the widespread belief in the industry that 1980 would be Dustin Hoffman's year to receive the Best Actor Oscar long denied him.

So, Woods became a candidate for Best Supporting Actor, where the competition was perceived as Robert Duvall (for *Apocalypse Now*) and Melvin Douglas (for *Being There*). It was also felt that the supporting category was more hospitable to unknowns and outsiders. (Remember Richard Farnsworth? He was nominated in 1979 for his supporting performance in 1978's *Comes a Horseman*. Though he eventually lost, the winner was not exactly a household name, either—Christoper Walken for *The Deer Hunter*.)

Once Woods's target was sighted, there was one small matter to be considered before Avco could start their campaign to get him nominated. Call it interoffice politics or maybe common courtesy, but the executives felt that some attention had to be given to *The Onion Field*'s dark horses.

Even though Avco felt actors John Savage and Franklyn Seales had little chance of being nominated, ads would be placed in the trade papers touting them as well. Likewise, there would be ads for director Harold Becker and producer Walter Coblenz. (The producer is the one who accepts the Best Picture Award.) Naturally, the bulk of the trade ads would be for Woods; the ads for the others were tokens, designed to assure goodwill and also to communicate Avco's confidence in the film as a whole.

In Woods's case the ads (which cost $600 to $1,000 an issue per page) served a second purpose, too. They informed the Academy members that Woods wanted to be in the supporting category, rather than among the leads.

A problem for Woods arose when Hollywood's foreign press corps announced the nominees for their own awards, the Golden Globes. Woods found himself competing in the Best Actor category, against Al Pacino, Jack Lemmon, Jon Voight, and Dustin Hoffman (who won the award, and later, the Best Actor Oscar). Woods recalled being flattered at his inclusion in the ranks of these better-known actors, but he was also a little concerned that the Academy voters might be getting conflicting signals: The ads said he was best supporting actor, but the foreign press was saying that he might be the best actor.

The problem was that the nominations were, and continue to be, a write-in process. In addition to picking out the actors who gave the best performances of the preceding year, the members of the actors' branch (there are over 1,000) must also individually decide whether the actor was a lead or a supporting player. Often it is speculated that votes are split between the categories, leaving the actors who are in the running without enough votes in either category for a nomination. In considering his failure to be nominated, Woods advanced this theory, but a theory is all it will ever be, since the Academy's votes aren't made public.

Another element of Avco's campaign involved screenings. Though they planned to take advantage of all their Academy-allotted screening opportunities, they felt that the film still needed a commercial outlet. Since *The Onion Field* had had a fall 1979 release, by early 1980 it had all but vanished from even the neighborhood screens. To get a visible venue for the film, Avco put it into one of Westwood's smaller theaters and held it there for three weeks. They were able to do this by renting the theater—called four-walling the movie—for a flat weekly fee. Academy members could get in free by showing their Academy membership card at the ticket window.

Still another element in Woods's Oscar quest was Woods himself. Here, too, Avco had a problem. It wasn't the actor's unwillingness to talk, but instead, his tendency to say too much.

For example, during an interview with *Los Angeles* magazine in late summer 1979 Woods broke a number of Hollywood conventions, first by questioning the intelligence of the people who then ran the studios, next by insulting some of his fellow actors, calling them "walking surfboards" by name, and finally by dumping on the Los Angeles life-style, which, as he saw it, paled in comparison with New York. He even managed to call the swank restaurant in which the interview took place a "Beverly Hills shithouse."

Fortunately for Woods, his Oscar campaign had not yet begun. When it did, some of the people at Avco cautioned Woods. " 'Jimmy,' I said," recalled one executive, " 'there's a time and a place for that, and now isn't the time.' "

Apparently heeding that advice, Woods did not let his anti-industry candor carry over to his appearances on "The Tonight Show." In December 1979 his appearance on the show was prefaced by a mention of his Oscar potential in his introduction by Johnny Carson. Woods then sat through two segments of the show speaking very quickly and punctuating his anecdotes with nervous laughter. Later, he would deny that he had been particularly uncomfortable. Carson apparently felt that, nervous or not, Woods was an interesting guest and promptly invited him back, this time for mid January—which happened to be during the Academy's nominating period. During this second appearance, Carson explored Woods's pro–New York sentiments, which Woods managed to express without ever denigrating Hollywood. Mostly, he emphasized his fascination with New York's eccentrics.

One small part of the campaign was probably the final nail in Woods's coffin. The ads that Avco ran in the trades for the Oscars used artwork similar to the ads used to attract people to the film itself. But added to the trade ads was a line that read, "Against all odds, a very independent film." The line was inserted by Wambaugh himself, probably with jaw jutted, as a way of vindicating himself before the community which had, as he often publicly complained, wrecked both his *New Centurions* and *The Choirboys* when transforming them from books into movies.

Avco was not pleased. The words *independent* and *against all odds* were direct affronts to the studios and thus an affront to the Academy's oldest and most established voters. Worse, they were delivered by someone who was a novice in the business. Wambaugh insisted on the lines, though, and Avco went along with him, in large part because they were looking forward to distributing his next film, *The Black Marble.*

"Joe said he was sorry about that, that he thought that was what lost it for me," commented Woods. His failure to be nominated left Woods more bemused than embittered. "What can I say? It's a crapshoot. Sure, I wanted to get it. I'll probably get one when I'm seventy for being in a movie about a burning building. And it won't be a regular Oscar, either. It'll be one of those special ones, like the Jean Hersholt Humanitarian Award or something.

"And who did win, anyway? That says it all, doesn't it? Three months later and nobody remembers." (It was Melvyn Douglas, for the role of Ben in *Being There.*)

16

THE FUTURE:

IS THE RISK GONE?

LISTEN TO MOST OF THE SPECULATIONS AND RUMORS MAKING THE rounds of the movie industry. The impression dawns with the subtlety of an automobile accident that utopia is waiting just around the corner. Evolving technology (cable and pay television systems, video cassettes, video disks), new financing sources and structures (investment offerings by the studios, the high profile adopted by banks and other lending institutions), and trailblazing into other kinds of performing arts (legitimate theater) all seem to connect up to describe a future era in which the element of risk will soon be as obsolete as the nickelodeon. The main knot holding the optimistic web of expectations together is the advent of cable and pay television.

Cable and pay television involve two separate categories. There is, first of all, the "hardware," or the cables, satellites, and decoder boxes. Then there is the "software," or, put simply, the material that is played on the hardware. Despite the fundamental fact that the production of hardware and the production of software are two distinct enterprises, the two obviously depend intimately on each other.

Studio folks like to use the compression *pay-cable* quite a bit, but that hyphen may be a little confusing, since payment is ubiquitous while the cable is not. For a long time, cable television was literally a backwoods operation that carried the signals of commercial stations over wires to paying rural viewers who would have to install antennas rivaling the NORAD system in order to get a good picture on the tube. In 1975 Home Box Office, owned by Time, Inc., leased an RCA satellite in order to get its for-pay programming out to the cable systems it owned. Almost overnight, a new industry was born. Cable television covered a continent instead of a county; even people with good television reception were signing up in order to see sports events and movies all presented without commercials.

Another form of pay television comes into homes via ultrahigh frequency (UHF) transmissions, which are broadcast in a scrambled form and decoded at the television set by a converter box. Industry insiders lump these two forms together under the "pay-cable" rubric.

The major reason for industry optimism about pay-cable is the size of the audience. About 16 million homes now have some form of pay-cable, a number expected to double by the middle of the decade. That prediction pegs the total number of cable subscribers at 30 million by 1985, or a penetration of somewhere around 35 to 40 percent of all the homes that currently own a television. (Revenues from "basic cable"—in other words, the money subscribers pay to get cable or pay—now total around $3 billion, and mid-decade predictions forecast revenue as high as $7 billion.)

Thirty million people. As a potential audience for films, that number is a giddy prospect indeed. Moviemakers are working out all sorts of profit arithmetic and giggling maniacally; all the equations would take a separate volume just to list. But here's one set of figures that puts the implications of pay-cable into relief: The average cost of making a studio film, we have noted, is now hovering around $10 million. Imagine that just one pay or cable subscription TV household in three tunes in that movie, either for a per-program payment or as part of a monthly fee. Imagine further that however that money is collected, it translates to around $2 per person. That's 10 million people at two bucks a throw, or a cool $20 million. Tack on the fact that the necessary $5 million minimum cost to promote a film actively need not be spent (only one print is supplied to the pay or cable company, and there is virtually no advertising, except on the cable or pay system itself), and the film goes into profit—$12 million worth—virtually overnight.

Here we have at last come to the intersection of hardware and software. The consumer pays for a pay-cable system. The people who operate that system have to have something to show to the consumer. While many consumers want sporting events or stock market advice, most want movies. As reporter Les Brown said in the *New York Times*, the expansion of pay-cable "is directly related to the consumer demand for the channels that deliver the newly released movies, uncut and without commercials, into the homes."

A similar intersection of software and hardware occurs in what is called the video business but is actually video cassettes and video disks. Basically, the consumer today has a choice of two videotape cassette systems on the market and two kinds of video disk players. Videotape machines accommodate a video cassette that can record or play back programming taken from the television set. Video disk systems are confined to the playback function. They utilize prerecorded disks that are "read" by either a laser or a diamond stylus similar to those used on conventional record players. Cassettes sell anywhere from $60 to $125 for prerecorded programming; disks are set to hit the market at $5.95 to $24.95. Here, too, the intersection of hardware and software creates enormous profit potential. As giant Japanese companies (Sony and Matsuchita, marketed under Panasonic) vie for a share of the videotape market, Phillips, MCA (in partnership with IBM), and RCA are scrambling for a piece of the disk domain. These corporate behemoths manufacture the system(s), and many other companies make prerecorded tapes or disks. They need something to show on them in order to appeal to consumers. They need software, and the prime candidate is of course movies.

The fundamental question of what cable-pay and video mean to future film distribution is one almost everyone in the industry tends to be tight-lipped about. Most frankly admit that they're not sure. The fact is that the complex ties and challenges posed by an awesomely lucrative home marketplace of video and pay-cable will clearly create problems in marketing. Many people are even afraid that the home market will eliminate moviegoing altogether, since they argue that there will no longer be a reason to go to a show.

Our own view takes a kind of middle course. As the cost of signing up for pay-cable or buying a video machine decreases, so also will the overall demand for movies shown in a theater. The reasons are obvious: The cost will be about the same, the convenience considerably maximized by staying at home. (Especially with the suburbs blighted with multiplex theaters, often no more than concrete blockhouses with a seven-foot screen and sound fidelity that is inferior to a middling home stereo system.)

Our guess is that two separate audiences for films will be created: The first is a group made up of older people, who once went to movies but now tend increasingly to stay at home. Bored with the monopoly programming of the three networks, they will subscribe to pay-cable as an alternative. The second group will look basically the same as the people who go to see films now. They will be younger, neither content to sit at home nor convinced by the inaccurate claim that a movie on TV is just the same as a movie in the theater. Simultaneous release patterns will probably not change the way either of these two groups approach films, although the older stay-at-homes will most likely become more sophisticated and selective in their movie tastes. They may even decide that the next time a movie starring an actor who they first saw and liked on pay-cable comes to the local theater, they'll go to see it, thinking, optimistically, perhaps the habit of going to movies instead of going to just a single movie will be reborn.

As for the pessimistic side of the crystal ball, it's hard to discover any really threatening clouds.* Economists tend to note that new demands are created in many cases simply by the appearance of new products on the market. The presence of home entertainment hard-

*Smaller theater owners are, however, directly threatened.

ware means that people will decide to buy them and in turn demand programming for these new purchases.

Although it is outside the scope of this book to assess the impact of these developments on network television, network executives are rightfully concerned. With 125-channel cable only a few years away, the television owner will have a dizzying number of options to choose among. He will choose what to watch, rather than let the networks make that choice for him. Even more provocatively, whereas it has long been lamented that a good network show that draws "only" 15 million viewers is considered a failure, a pay-cable event needs to attract only 2 or 3 million people to be a financial success. In prerecorded video form, sales need to be even less. Therefore, it should come as no surprise that the networks, too, are moving into programming for pay-cable and home video.

Perhaps the major minus of the film industry's rush to home entertainment will be seen in the films themselves. The artistic choices TV directors and writers make are fundamentally different from those made by feature directors and writers. Broad vistas lose much of their impact on the small screen, so they may be avoided. So will wide-screen compositions, since the TV tube cuts off fully half of the wide-screen image. In film tight close-ups are used sparingly because they have so much impact on the thirty-foot screen; on TV, close-ups have a more reasonable proportion. Expect more of them—and more dialogue to go with them—as film directors and writers gear their styles more toward what could be their primary venue, the small screen.

But the loss of visual subtleties will be nothing in comparison with other changes. Because of the way they are presented, movies have a visceral impact that cannot be equaled by anything shown on television. Unlike TV, movies in theaters demand our attention and magnify their subjects. As movies are "videofied," the impact of all films will be diminished, but especially hurt will be the action and horror genres, since much of their threat and shock value will be defused. Expect more talk to replace action.

Finally, there's a more ephemeral issue: We tend to expect more of what we see on the big screen than of what we see on television.

Television has always been that box in the living room that we may "watch" while eating, reading, or conversing. Consequently, its programs were never expected to meet very stringent artistic standards. That doesn't necessarily mean that movies are always better than TV, but it does mean that the features of the future might be subjected to less rigorous critical standards.

Pay-cable and home video are also having a catalytic effect on the financing of films. Indeed, a recent headline in the *Hollywood Reporter* went so far as to say: "WALL ST. EMBRACING FILM CO.'S NOW THAT RISK IS VIRTUALLY GONE." But home entertainment is only part of the picture. In a sense, it is an attractive "extra" to the business practices now being carried out in the more traditional realm of theatrical distribution. Guarantees from theater owners and overseas distributors enable many a movie to be made without the investment of a single penny by the studio or independent producer. Some movies have gone into profit prior to release, thanks to guarantee payments.

One studio, 20th Century-Fox, is so confident of the security of a film investment that it offered equity positions in its film production for the first time in 1980. Announced through a prospectus issued by the Wall Street brokers A. G. Becker, Inc., the investment program was made up of 128 individual units selling for $150,000 a slice. Investors were asked to gamble 25 percent of the total production at Fox for about eighteen months, in return for an equal stake in the profits, including all home entertainment and free TV sales. This kind of "private placement," used prevalently in other businesses, is a new concept in the movie industry. It was eagerly embraced.

As for banks, one trade paper described the rush to loan money to the film business as an inelegant race, where "the nation's banks are falling over one another to get a piece of the action." Some, like Bank of America, Union Bank, and First National Bank of Boston, are respected outfits, doubly regarded in these profitable days by virtue of the fact that they also made money available in the leaner years of the late 1960s and early 1970s. However, announcements of "entertainment business seminars" crowd the pages of the trade papers as other banks reach out with loan deals for new customers. The reasons may begin with the glamour and prestige of association with the movies, but they end with considerations of pure profit. Writing a loan on a successful film or underwriting a production schedule at a studio may be no more profitable than loans to other kinds of businesses. But the point is that movies are today perceived as safe enough investments for banks to engage in. The banks add new loan customers, and increased income from interest on new loans.

Heightened participation by the investment community in films has made possible the entry of some of the studios into full-time legitimate theater subsidiaries. Columbia and Warners, in particular (*Dancin'* and *The Duchess of Duke Street*, respectively), have been active on Broadway. The hope is that the stage will serve as both a development site and a presale mechanism for properties that can later be made into films or offered exclusively to pay-cable and video—or both.

It is clear, first of all, that the movie business will very quickly become a landscape of potentially immense profit. Blessed with a hit film, the take could be staggering. Even at a combined cost for production and promotion of, say, $30 million, a smash could become almost a perpetual revenue machine. Foreign distribution brings in millions. Pay-cable adds to the pot, along with video sales in cassette or on disc. All of this in *addition* to earnings at the box office. One hundred million dollars of income could be generated from even a moderately popular film; incomes of a quarter of a billion dollars per film could be captured by blockbusters.

The voracious appetites of the new hardware systems should also prove to be an effective buffer against loss. The entire negative cost of film may not be collected, but a significant dent can be made. And, if all else fails, a large cash flow from a hit can float even the most expensive flop.

Nor is it only the studios that will benefit. Independent producers tend to have expensive film catalogues of "R"-rated material that would have been a total loss just a few years ago. Unable to generate excitement at the box office, more than a bit too gamy for television, these same films can be sold to cable or pay operators. Menahem Golan, one of the founders of the independent Cannon Group, has said that inquiries to his company have increased some 400 percent from cable operators in the United States—all concerning titles that were precluded by their rating or subject matter from sales to free TV.

It adds up to a brand-new sales avenue for moviemakers and movie distributors. Every one of the studios has formed and funded a home entertainment division to explore and exploit new cable and video markets. Although its formation is being challenged in the courts by the Department of Justice (citing violation of the consent decrees discussed in an earlier chapter of this book), the intended launching by four major studios and Getty Oil of a cable system of their own shows the level of industry excitement. At the same time, Home Box Office has begun to produce programming of its own to supply its cable system. The programming price tag for their first year of production is a reported $20 million. Their closest competitor, Showtime, has committed $15 million.

A conclusion seems inescapable that the nature of movie-going is in for some changes. Some studios are openly discussing a practice that would have been taboo only last year: simultaneous release of movies at the box office and on pay-cable. Complicating matters still further, 20th Century-Fox has announced their intention to market home video cassette versions of theatrical motion pictures simultaneously with theatrical releases. Fox executives have also announced a program of *first-run* production for the home video market. "It's not as crazy as it sounds at first," an industry observer told us. "In fact, it's not crazy at all. It costs twenty bucks to go to a movie, park the car, pay the sitter. You can buy a new movie on disk for twenty-five dollars. Why not?"

The conclusion that leaps out from this survey of the immediate future for films is that the movie business is entering an epochal era.

One of the ways we have been examining the film industry is to look at the enterprise as a risky undertaking in which a number of techniques are employed to soften the risk. Tomorrow it appears that our conception will be inapplicable. Cash on hand or loan commitments are now more than equal to the money needed for production, although the indies still must scramble. Home entertainment seems certain to attract even more investment interest, and it will dramatically increase the profitability of hits and minimize the losses incurred by flops. Home entertainment will also reach back into the past, turning film classics in the vaults into hot items on cable, disk, or tape.

So, it might reasonably be asked: Where is the risk?

In general, we are convinced that risk is still very much a part of getting the picture of how the movie business works. Film has always been an unknown quantity. Several inalterable facets of film bear repeating. Film cannot be tested in the market until it has been released. Hence the axiom that there is no way to tell ahead of time if a film will succeed or fail. A star can join the cast, a sequel can be produced. Either may fail while an unheralded movie takes off like a rocket. Meanwhile the theater owners who have staked a guarantee, the distributors abroad who have rendered up-front money, and the merchandisers who buy licenses will all lose money on the failure. Or they may be too late to get in on the profits from the surprise hit. It is true that the company that produced or distributed the costly bomb may now be protected from loss through pay-cable or video, but others in the industry are not. They, at least, lose.

Additionally, a film that nobody likes is a film that nobody likes. We can paraphrase Gertrude Stein to say that a bomb is a bomb is a bomb. A bomb on cable, a bomb down at the video cassette store, a bomb at the box office. A big-budget disaster, to which all of these entities have contributed money, will mean that that money will be lost. As the potential for spiraling profits increases, so, too, does an equally widespread financial disaster become a possibility.

Another factor in the analysis of risk is the stubborn tendency of people in Hollywood to lag behind in their understanding of new technology. Sound was resisted, as was color. Television was perceived exclusively as a threat. Now, since producers and distributors are fanning the fires of enthusiasm for pay-cable and home video, it might appear that at last they have aligned their outlook with available technology. Unfortunately, this seems to be only partly so. It is true enough that the leaders of the industry have grasped the moneymaking promise held out by new technology. But the blockbuster mentality still clings. "The big movie" generating a tidal wave of cash is still the dream. Nowhere is the capability of cable to appeal to very specific, discreet audiences being talked about as a way to insure a continued place for smaller, more personal films. And the disastrous summer of 1980 pointed out that a secure financial footing meant only that the moguls were unafraid of the fiscal effects of turning out an unprecedented collection of utter garbage. About eighty movies—thirty more than the year before—were released then, evidently on the theory that if one didn't work, the next one might. The hits among them can be counted easily on two hands. Just because the money was there to make films, films were made, it seemed. Many of them deserved to make money but were given only a week to sink or swim, since the next film in line had to be exhibited.

The greatest risk has now become the risk that producers and distributors take through a policy of indiscriminate production accomplished at top speed. Certainly, the financial losses can be partly made up through ancillary rights deals, or the debt service on a loan paid off by the next successful horror or sci-fi epic. But in the process, the public starts to believe that movies in general are deteriorating, regardless of the form in which they are presented. A time of great promise for the film industry has therefore quickly become the period of its greatest peril.

INDEX

ABOUT THE AUTHORS

DAVID LEES resides in San Clemente, California, and serves as an advertising consultant and copywriter to a number of large nonprofit institutions. He has published widely on a variety of topics related to art, media, and money for *New West*, *Los Angeles*, *Coast*, *Los Angeles Times Book Review*, the *UCLA Monthly*, *Art Week*, and *Surfer*.

STAN BERKOWITZ studied film production and screenwriting at UCLA. He began writing about film for the *UCLA Daily Bruin* and later wrote articles for *Film Comment*, *Coast*, the West Coast supplement of *Rolling Stone*, the Los Angeles *Times*, *US*, and *Box Office*. He was once a grip on the crew of Russ Meyer's *The Supervixens* and now works in the field of film restoration. A native of Los Angeles, he currently lives in Santa Monica, California.

VINTAGE CRITICISM: LITERATURE, MUSIC, AND ART

VINTAGE FICTION, POETRY, AND PLAYS